DIAGRAM SHOWING HOW WE GOT OUR BIBLE

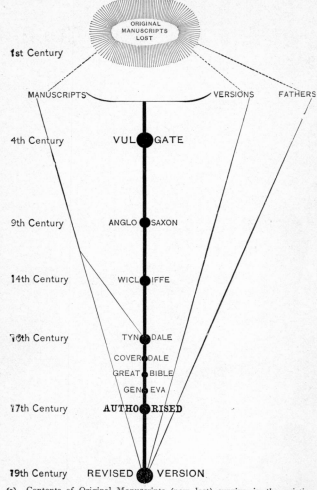

(1) Contents of Original Manuscripts (now lost) survive in the existing MANUSCRIPTS, VERSIONS, and FATHERS. (See p. 10.)

(2) The Latin Vulgate (a revision of the Old Latin *Versions* by comparison with Greek and Hebrew *Manuscripts*) is the source of our English Versions down to Tyndale. He first draws from *manuscript* sources but of modern date.

(3) The three sources—MANUSCRIPTS, VERSIONS, and FATHERS—are all combined for the first time in the recent Revision.

How We Got Our Bible

BY

J. PATERSON SMYTH

B.D., LL.D., LITT.D., D.C.L.

*Author of "The Bible in the Making," "How God Inspired the
Bible," "The Ancient Documents and the Modern Bible,"
"How to Read the Bible," "The Story of St.
Paul's Life and Letters,"*

NEW YORK
JAMES POTT & CO.
1922

New and Revised Edition, April, 1912
Reprinted Jan. and Dec., 1913
    "   Feb., 1914
    "   Oct., 1915
    "   Jan. and Dec., 1916
    "   Oct., 1917
    "   Feb. and Nov., 1919
    "   Nov., 1920
    "   Oct., 1921
    "   May, 1922

CONTENTS.

iii

CONTENTS.

CHAPTER V.

WYCLIFFE'S VERSION.

CHAPTER VI.

TYNDALE'S VERSION.

CHAPTER VII.

THE BIBLE AFTER TYNDALE'S DAYS.

CHAPTER VIII.

THE REVISED VERSION.

LIST OF ILLUSTRATIONS.

v

HOW WE GOT OUR BIBLE

CHAPTER I.

SOURCES OF OUR BIBLE.

I. The Old Record Chest. II. Copyists' Errors. III. Necessity of Revision. IV. Sources of Information open to Revisers. V. Textual Criticism.

LET the scope of this book be clearly understood. The question How we got our Bible is a very wide one and the full answer should tell of the making of the Bible and the writers of the Books and the ancient historical material which they used and also how it happened that this particular collection of books came to be separated from the other literature of the time and regarded as inspired and collected into a Bible. This part of the answer I have already tried to give in another book.

The present treatise takes the answer at a later stage when the books were already completed and received as the inspired guide of the Church. It traces the story of the Bible from the early manuscripts of Apostolic days down to the last Revised Version which is in our hands to-day.[1]

I.

We begin by imagining before us the record chest of one of the early Christian churches,—say Jerusalem, or Rome, or Ephesus,—about 120 A. D., when sufficient time had elapsed since the completion of the New Testament writings to allow most of the larger churches to procure copies for themselves. In any one church, perhaps, we should not find very much, but if we collect together the documents of some of the leading churches we should have before us something of this sort:

[1]The writer has issued a full series of books on the making of the Bible which should be read, as far as possible, in the order stated:

I. THE BIBLE IN THE MAKING.
　　　in the light of modern research.
　　This is the book referred to on previous page.

II. HOW WE GOT OUR BIBLE.

III. THE ANCIENT DOCUMENTS AND THE MODERN BIBLE.
　　　An easy lesson for the people on textual criticism; with plates and fac-similes.

IV. HOW GOD INSPIRED THE BIBLE.
　　　Thoughts for the present disquiet about Higher Criticism.

V. HOW TO READ THE BIBLE.
　　　Suggestions on reading the Divine Library.

VI. THE STORY OF ST. PAUL'S LIFE AND LETTERS.

I. Some manuscripts of the Hebrew Old Testament books.

> The reader will keep in mind that the Old Testament books were originally written in Hebrew, those of the New Testament in Greek.

II. A good many more of the Old Testament books translated into Greek for general use in the churches, Greek being the language most widely known at the time.

> This translation is called the Septuagint, or " Version of the Seventy," from an old tradition of its having been prepared by seventy learned Jews of Alexandria. It was made at different times, beginning somewhere about 280 B. C., and was the version commonly used by the Evangelists and Apostles. This accounts for the slight difference we sometimes notice between the Old Testament and their quotations from it, our Old Testament being translated direct from the Hebrew.

III. A few rolls of the Apocryphal Books, written by holy men in the Church, and valued for the practical teaching they contained.

IV. Copies of the Gospels and the Acts, the Epistles of SS. Paul and Peter and John, and the Book of the Revelation.

II.

Now let us remember clearly that as we look into that old record chest of nearly 1800 years ago, we have before us all the sources from which we get our Bible.

And remember further that these writings were

of course all manuscript, *i. e.*, written by the hand, and that copies when needed had each to be written out, letter by letter, at a great expense of time and trouble, and of course, very often too at some expense of the original correctness.   However careful the scribe might be, it was almost impossible, in copying a long and difficult manuscript, to prevent the occurrence of errors.   Sometimes he would mistake one letter for another—sometimes, if having the manuscript read to him, he would confound two words of similar sound—sometimes after writing in the last word of a line, on looking up again his eye would catch the same word at the end of the next line, and he would go on from that, omitting the whole line between.   Remarks and explanations, too, written in the margin might sometimes in transcribing get inserted in the text.

In these and various other ways errors might creep into the copy of his manuscript.   These errors would be repeated by the man that afterward copied from this, who would also sometimes add other errors of his own.   So that it is evident, as copies increased, the errors would be likely to increase with them, and therefore, as a general rule,[1] THE EARLIER ANY MANUSCRIPT, THE MORE LIKELY IT IS TO BE CORRECT.

[1] This is only a general rule. Of course it is quite possible for a manuscript A. D. 1500 to be copied *direct* from one of A. D. 300, and therefore to be more correct than some a thousand years older.

The reader may easily test this for himself by copying a dozen pages of a book, then hand on the copy to a friend to recopy, and let him pass on to another what he has written, and so have the operation repeated through six or eight different hands before comparing the last copy with the original. It will be an interesting illustration of the danger of errors in copying. Even in printed Bibles, whose proofs have been carefully examined and reëxamined, these mistakes creep in. To take two examples out of many: An edition published in 1653, reads 1 Cor. vi. 9, " Know ye not that the unrighteous shall inherit the kingdom of God; " and the " Printer's Bible," much sought by book collectors, puts the strange anachronism in King David's mouth, " Printers have persecuted me without a cause " (Ps. cxix. 161).

We know, of course, God might have miraculously prevented scribes and compositors from making these mistakes; but it does not seem to be God's way anywhere to work miracles for us where our own careful use of the abilities He has given would suffice for the purpose.

III.

Although, owing to the special care exercised in transcribing the Scriptures,[1] the errors would be in most cases of comparatively trifling importance, yet it is evident from what has been said about the growth of copyists' errors, that in the course of the centuries before the invention of printing, Bible manuscripts might easily have grown very faulty indeed. Therefore the printed Bibles, taken hastily from these modern and probably corrupt manuscripts, would need a thorough revision, and this revision would need to be repeated again and again, as facilities increased, till the Scriptures were as nearly as possible as they left the inspired writers' hands.

But how is this revision to be accomplished? Of course, if the original writings had remained, it would be quite a simple operation, as a careful comparison with them would at any time discover whatever had need of correction. But, it is hardly

---

[1] As an interesting instance of the care exercised in transcribing important documents, Irenæus, Bishop of Lyons, in the second century, thus writes in one of his own books: "Whosoever thou art who shalt transcribe this book, I charge thee with an oath by our Lord Jesus Christ, and by His glorious appearing, in which He cometh to judge the quick and dead, that thou carefully compare what thou hast transcribed, and correct it according to this copy whence thou hast transcribed it, and thou transcribe this oath in like manner, and place it in thy copy." Farther on I shall have to notice the solemn reverential care bestowed by the Hebrew scribes on copies of the Old Testament.

necessary to say, the original writings have long
since disappeared.   Some of them, written on the
common writing material of the day,—the papyrus
paper referred to in 2 John, ver. 12,—very soon
got worn out from use,[1] others were lost or destroyed in the early Christian persecutions.   In
any case they have totally disappeared.

How then is revision to be accomplished?   In
the absence of these original manuscripts, what
sources of information are open to Bible revisers?

IV.

For answer let us turn from the ancient record
chest, whose contents are now irrecoverably lost,
and imagine beneath some oaken library roof a
vast mass of manuscripts, piled up before us in
THREE separate heaps,—manuscripts of very
varied kind—stained and torn old parchments—
books of faded purple, lettered with silver—beautifully designed ornamental pages—bundles of fine
vellum, yellow with age, bright even yet with the
gold and vermilion laid on by pious hands a thousand years since—in many shapes, in many
colours, in many languages,—thousands of old
Scripture writings reaching back for 1500 years.

---

[1] Jerome tells of such a library in Cæsarea, already partly
destroyed within a century after its formation, and of the en-
deavors of two presbyters to restore the manuscripts by copying
them on parchment.

This pile represents the great Biblical treasures stored up to-day in the various libraries of Europe —all the old copies at present remaining of the inspired Books. And here in this mass of old manuscripts is the material accessible to scholars for the purpose of Bible revision.

In these piles we shall find three different classes of writings: (1) These faded parchments, with the crowded square lettering, are *copies in the original languages* of the different Scriptures contained in the old record chest. These are known as Biblical " MANUSCRIPTS," for though all the early Scriptures are of course written by the hand, the name *manuscripts* has been by common consent of scholars appropriated to the *copies in the original tongue.*

(2) But those farther on are evidently different in language, the writing, at least of the few whose pages are visible, being so very unlike the others. That open manuscript on the top, written all over in running lines and loops, is a Syriac translation, the two next are Coptic and Latin, and all these are ANCIENT VERSIONS, *i. e., translations of the Bible* into the languages of early Christendom, some of them representing the Scriptures of about fifty years after the death of St. John.

(3) The contents of the third pile, though a good deal resembling the Biblical manuscripts in appearance, are not even books of the Scriptures

at all, but WRITINGS OF THE EARLY CHRISTIAN FATHERS from the second to the fifth century. The use of these we shall see afterwards.

V.

The science that deals with this mass of evidence is called " textual criticism," a science which, though only in its infancy when our Authorized Version was issued, has reached in the present day a very high degree of perfection. Suppose then our revisers, men skilled in this study, are occupied on say a passage in the Epistle to the Romans, desiring to present it as nearly as possible as it left the hands of St. Paul, how will they make use of this mass of evidence?

I. They will search for the *very oldest Greek manuscripts* in which the Epistle occurs, for, as we have already seen, the oldest are likely to be the most correct, and they will get *as many as possible* of them to compare them together for the eliminating any errors that may have crept in, for it is evident that if a number of copies are made of the same original, even should each of the copyists have erred, no two are likely to make exactly the same error, therefore a false reading in any one can often be corrected by comparison with the others.

II. Then they will examine the *ancient versions*, and see how the passage in question was read in Syriac and Latin and other ancient languages 1700 years ago.

III. But what use can they make of the rest of the parchments—those writings of the early Christian Fathers? A very important use. They search these carefully for quotations from this Epistle. These early Fathers quoted Scripture so largely in their controversies that it has been said if all the other sources of the Bible were lost, we could recover the greater part of it from their writings. The most important of them lived in the second, third, and fourth centuries, and as they of course quote from the Scriptures in use in their time, it is like going back sixteen hundred years to ask men, How did your Scripture render this passage of St. Paul? Unfortunately their quotations seem often made from memory, which a good deal spoils the value of their testimony.

The sources of information, then, open to revisers may be briefly summed up as—

I. Manuscripts. II. Versions. III. Quotations from the Fathers.[1] Each of these will be treated of more fully in the following chapters.

[1] See Diagram facing the title-page.

PHOTOGRAPH OF ANCIENT GREEK MANUSCRIPTS:

(From Westwood's *Paleographia Sacra Pictoria*.)

1. Scrap of a famous Greek Manuscript of Genesis, (Codex Geneseos Cottonianus).

2. Portions of its writing, full size.

3. Fac-simile of the Alexandrian Codex in the British Museum.

4. A portion of a 9th Century Manuscript.

5. Beginning of 29th Psalm on Papyrus in the British Museum

CHAPTER II.

ANCIENT MANUSCRIPTS.

The Oldest Bibles in the World. I. The Vatican Manuscript. II. The Sinaitic Manuscript. III. The Alexandrian. IV. Palimpsests. V. The Manuscript of Beza. VI. Cursive Manuscripts. VII. Old Testament Revision.

LET us still keep imaged before our minds the triple pile of Biblical writings to be examined.

We come first to the MANUSCRIPTS, the *copies* [1] of the Scripture in the original tongues. Of the Greek there is quite a large number—more than 1500—before us, and from the difference in their condition and general appearance one is inclined to suspect that they must vary a good deal in age, and therefore probably in value. The question of determining the age of a manuscript is a very intricate one; but it should make our inspection of these the more interesting if I briefly state a few easy marks to guide us:

The form of the letters is the chief guide. The oldest and therefore most valuable are written in

[1] The reader should keep this distinction clearly before him to prevent confusion. MANUSCRIPTS=copies in the original tongue. VERSIONS=translations into other tongues.

capital letters, and without any division between the words, as if we should write

NOWWHENJ͞SWASBORNINBETHLEHEMOFJ.
These are called *uncial* manuscripts. The modern are written in a running hand like our writing, and are therefore called *cursive*. (It will be useful to remember these names, as they frequently occur in Bible commentaries, and in criticisms of the Revised Version.)

Then again, initial letters, miniatures, and in general any ornamentation of manuscripts, marks them as of comparatively late date.

Far the greater number of the manuscripts before us are written in the cursive hand, many of them beautifully illuminated and ornamented with exquisite miniatures and initials. But we turn at once from these to their less attractive companions, those few faded, worn parchments with the old uncial letters. Notice especially those three bound in square book form; they are plain, faded-looking documents, with little about them to attract attention, but these three manuscripts are among the greatest treasures the Christian Church possesses—the oldest copies of the Bible in the world! They are named respectively the Vatican, Sinaitic, and Alexandrian Manuscripts. They have been largely used in the recent Bible Revision, *but they were not any of them accessible to*

*those who prepared the Authorized Version in
1611.*

These three oldest manuscripts are curiously
enough in possession of the three great branches
of the Christian Church.   The ALEXANDRIAN
(called for shortness *Codex* A) belongs to Protestant England, and is kept in the manuscript room
of the British Museum; the VATICAN (*Codex* B)
is in the Vatican Library at Rome; and the
SINAITIC (*Codex* Aleph), which has only lately
been discovered, is one of the treasures of the
Greek Church at St. Petersburg.

These manuscripts show us the Bible as it existed soon after the apostolic days.   There has
been a good deal of discussion about their age,
which need not be entered on here; but we shall
not be far from the truth if we say roundly that
they range from about 300 to 450 A. D.   Therefore the oldest is about as distant in time from
the original inspired writings as the Revised is
from the Authorized Version.   All the Greek
manuscripts before this time seem to have perished
in the terrible persecutions which were directed
not only against the Christians themselves, but
also and with special force against their sacred
writings.

I.

THE VATICAN MANUSCRIPT. Each of these three manuscripts has its history. The most ancient, it is generally agreed, is the Vatican manuscript, which has lain at least four or five hundred years in the Vatican Library at Rome. One is much inclined to grudge the Roman Church the possession of this our most valuable manuscript; for the papal authorities have been very jealous guardians, and most persons capable of examining it aright have been refused access to it. Dr. Tregelles, one of our most eminent students of textual criticism, made an attempt; but he says they would not let him open the volume without searching his pockets, and depriving him of pens and ink and paper; the two priests told off to watch him would try to distract his attention if he seemed too intent on any passage, and if he studied any part of it too long they would snatch away the book. However, it has of late years become easily accessible through the excellent fac-similes made by order of Pope Pius IX., which may be seen in our chief public libraries.

The manuscript consists of about 700 leaves of the finest vellum, about a foot square, bound together in book form. It is not quite perfect, having lost Gen. i.–xlvi., as well as Psalms cv.–

cxxxvii., and all after Heb. ix. 14 of the New Testament. The original writing must have been beautifully delicate and finely formed. There are only a few words left here and there by which to judge of this; for from one end to the other, the whole manuscript has been travelled over by the pen of some meddlesome scribe of about the tenth century. Probably he was afraid of the precious writing fading out if it were not thus inked over; but if so his fears were quite groundless, for here are some of the words which he passed over (considering them incorrect) remaining still perfectly clear and legible after the lapse of 1500 years. Each page contains three colums, and the writing is in capital letters, without any division between the words. This makes it less easy to read, but of course it was done to save space at a time when writing material was very expensive.

To carry this saving further, words are written smaller and more crowded as they approach the end of a line, and for the same reason was adopted the plan of contracted words, which has often been the cause of manuscript errors. First, they cut off the final M's and N's at the end of a word, marking the omission by a line across the top, as if we should write LONDO for London; then they proceeded to the dropping of final syllables, and from that to the shortening of frequently recurring words, like the name Jesus or God. We might fairly represent these peculiarities (which are common to all the early manuscripts) by writing thus in English (Titus ii. 11, 12):

FORTHEGRACEOF G͞D BRINGing
SALVATIONHATHAPPEARED
TOALL M͞N TEACHINGUSTHATDEN
YINGUNGODLINESSANDWOR
LDLYLUSTWESHOULDLIVESOB
ERLYANDGODLYINTHISPRESENT
EVILWORLDLOOKINGFORTHAT

One remark more before we lay it aside. It will be noticed that in the Revised New Testament the passage at the end of St. Mark's Gospel is printed in as in some degree doubtful, with a note in the margin that "the two oldest Greek manuscripts omit these verses." Now this and the Sinaitic are the two manuscripts referred to, and if we could examine the manuscripts we should see that this one, while omitting the passage, curiously enough leaves a blank space for it on the page, showing that the scribe knew of its existence, but was undecided whether he should put it in or not.

II.

THE SINAITIC MANUSCRIPT. There is no need of describing this celebrated manuscript, which on the whole very much resembles the other; but the

THE SINAITIC MANUSCRIPT.

PHOTOGRAPH OF ONE OF THE SHEETS FOUND BY DR. TISCHENDORF IN THE OLD BASKET AT ST CATHARINE'S MONASTERY, MT. SINAI.

This sheet is an important witness on the controversy about the closing verses of St Mark's Gospel (See p. 27.)

story of its discovery about fifty years ago is full of interest. It is called the Sinaitic Manuscript from the place where it was found by the great German scholar, Dr. Tischendorf. His whole life was given up to the discovery and study of ancient manuscripts of the Bible, and he travelled all over the East, searching every old library he could get into for the purpose; but it was quite unexpectedly in St. Catharine's Convent, at the foot of Mount Sinai, that he discovered this the " pearl of all his researches," as he calls it.

In visiting the library of the convent in the month of May, 1844, he perceived in the middle of the great hall a basket full of old parchments, and the librarian told him that two heaps of similar old documents had already been used for the fires. What was his surprise to find in the basket a number of sheets of a copy of the Septuagint (Greek) Old Testament, the most ancient-looking manuscript that he had ever seen. The authorities of the convent allowed him to take away about forty sheets, as they were only intended for the fire; but he displayed so much satisfaction with his gift that the suspicion of the monks was aroused as to the value of the manuscript, and they refused to give him any more.

He returned to Germany, and with his precious sheets made a great sensation in the literary world. But he took very good care not to tell where he had got them, as he still had hopes of securing the remainder; and he soon had reason to congratulate himself on his caution, for the English Government at once sent out a scholar to buy up any valuable Greek manuscripts he could lay hands on, and poor Dr. Tischendorf was very uneasy lest the Englishman should stumble upon the old basket on Mount Sinai. You may judge of his relief when he saw the Englishman's report soon after, telling of his failure; " for," said he, " after the visit of such a critic as Dr. Tischendorf, I could not, of course, expect any success." The doctor seems quite to enjoy the telling this part of the story.

He tried next, by means of an influential friend at the court of Egypt, to procure the rest of the manuscript, but without success. " The monks of the convent," wrote his friend, " have since your departure learned the value of the parchments, and now they will not part with them at any price." So he paid another visit to Mount Sinai, but could only find one sheet, containing eleven lines of the book of Genesis, which showed him that the manuscript originally contained the entire Old Testament.

To shorten the story, I must pass over fifteen years, during which time he had enlisted the sympathy of the Emperor of Russia, and in 1859 we find him again at the convent with a commission from the Emperor himself. However, he found very little of any value, and had made his arrangements to leave without accomplishing his mission, when a quite unexpected event brought about all that he had wished for. The very evening before he was to leave he was walking in the grounds with the steward of the convent, and as they returned the monk asked him into his cell to take some refreshment. Scarcely had they entered the cell, when, resuming his former conversation, the monk said: " I too have read a copy of that Septuagint." And so saying he took down a bulky bundle, wrapped in red cloth, and laid it on the table. Tischendorf opened the parcel, and to his great surprise found not only those very fragments that he had seen fifteen years before, but also other parts of the Old Testament, the New Testament complete, and some of the Apocryphal Books.

Full of joy, which this time he had the self-command to conceal, he asked in a careless way for permission to look over it in his bedroom. " And there by myself," he says, " I gave way to my transports of joy. I knew that I held in my hand one of the most precious Biblical treasures in existence, a document whose age and importance exceeded that of any I had ever seen after twenty years' study of the subject."

At length, through the Emperor's influence, he

succeeded in obtaining the precious manuscript, which is now stored up in the Library of St. Petersburg, the greatest treasure which the Eastern Church possesses. Strange that after all the vicissitudes of fifteen centuries it should at length be restored to the world only fifty years since! It is now easily accessible to scholars through its fac-similes in all our great libraries.

Now see the photographed sheet of this manuscript, at page —, shewing the close of St. Mark's gospel and the beginning of St. Luke's. We have purposely chosen this part of the manuscript for illustration. We have already (page 16) mentioned the fact that the Revised Version has printed the last twelve verses of St. Mark as in some degree doubtful, and has put a notice in the margin that "the two oldest Greek Manuscripts omit these verses." This and the Vatican Mauscript are the two referred to. The evidence of the Vatican manuscript, however, is very doubtful, for though it omits these verses it leaves the whole following column blank as well as the remainder of the column on which v. 8 is written. Nowhere else does it leave such a blank at the end of a book, and the fact indicates that the scribe knew of the existence of the passage and was uncertain whether to put it in or not.

The evidence of the Sinaitic, however, is quite unhesitating. St. Mark's gospel evidently ends on this page as photographed, and any one who can read Greek can see in this photograph that it ends with the words EPHOBOUNTO GAR, "for they were afraid" (v. 8).

It should be interesting for the reader to be able to see the very passage on which the Revisers depend so much. This is not the place to discuss the question whether the Revisers are right or not. But we may here say that those two old manuscripts with some statements of Eusebius, the great church historian, are the only important evidence against the passage in question, while nearly all the rest of the manuscripts and most of the Versions bear testimony on the other side.

III.

THE ALEXANDRIAN MANUSCRIPT (Codex A). This youngest of our three great manuscripts has special interest for us, being in the custody of England, and preserved with our great national treasures in the British Museum. It was presented to Charles I. by Cyril Lucar, Patriarch of Constantinople, A. D. 1628, and therefore arrived in England seventeen years too late to be of use in preparing our Authorized Version. The Arabic inscription on the first sheet, states that it was written "by the hand of Thekla the Martyr."

Only ten leaves are missing from the Old Testament part, but the New Testament is much more defective, having lost twenty-five leaves from the beginning of St. Matthew, two from St. John, and three from Corinthians. It is written two columns on a page, the Vatican and Sinaitic having respectively three and four. The original can be seen at the British Museum, but copies which exactly represent it are, like those of the other two, kept in our chief public libraries. A small piece of it has been photographed in the plate of the five Greek manuscripts. See plate facing page 10.

IV.

Here is the Codex of Ephraem, a very curious manuscript, all stained and soiled, and seemingly of little value, as it is written in quite a modern hand. It requires a closer examination to notice under that straggling handwriting the faint, faded lines of old uncial letters. This is what is called a Palimpsest or Rescript Manuscript, *i. e.,* one that has had its original contents rubbed out to make room for some other writing. We noticed already contractions, &c., adopted to save parchment at a time when it was very expensive. For the same purpose scribes sometimes used old parchments that had been written on before, and, by carefully scraping and pumicing out the old letters, made the skin tolerably fit for use again.

THE CODEX OF EPHRAEM.

NOTICE UNDER THE MODERN WRITING THE FAINTER LETTERS OF THE OLD BIBLE THAT HAD BEEN RUBBED OUT.

It need hardly be said that in many cases the writing thus blotted out was of far greater value than that which replaced it, and especially is it so in this case, where an ancient and valuable copy of the Scriptures was in the twelfth century coolly scrubbed out to make room for some theological discourses of St. Ephraem, an old Syrian Father.

The old writing, however, had not been so thoroughly rubbed but that some dim traces remained, which drew attention to the manuscript about 200 years since. It was very difficult to decipher the old hand till some chemical preparation applied in 1834 revived a good part of it, though it very much stained and defaced the vellum. The MS. was then found to contain a considerable portion of both Old and New Testaments, and it is considered almost if not quite as old as the Alexandrian. It was brought into France by Queen Catherine de Medici of evil memory and is now preserved in the Royal Library at Paris. A portion of it is reproduced on the opposite page.

V.

There is just one more uncial manuscript that deserves mention. This is the Codex Bezæ which is in the University Library at Cambridge. It was presented to the University in 1581, by Theodore Beza, the friend of Calvin, with a statement in his own handwriting that he had got it in 1562, from the monastery of St. Irenæus, at Lyons— (Lyons was sacked in that year). It is somewhat later in date than the other great uncials already mentioned and is written in Greek and Latin on opposite pages.

It is in many ways a curious and interesting document. It shows part of a very old Greek and a very old Latin Bible which do not always exactly correspond. It shows traces of the work of several correctors, some of them very ancient. One can see how the original scribe, whenever he made a slip, washed it out with a sponge, and how he corrected with a pen nearly empty of ink. Later correctors scraped out with a knife what seemed to them incorrect, and so have in some places spoiled the manuscript. But the most curious thing is the daring interpolations in the text, most of which are entirely unsupported by other manuscripts. Most of them are probably worthless but yet it is not improbable that some of them may contain lost sayings and deeds of Our Lord, such as St. John refers to in chapter xxi. 25, " there are also many other things which Jesus did, the which if they should be written every one I suppose that even the world itself would not contain the books that should be written."

Our photograph facing page 25, shows a very famous one, of which even so cautious a writer as

ΜΒ:
ΟΙΟΥΚΕΞΟΝΗΝΦΑΓΕΝΕΙΝΕΙΜΗΜΟΝΟΙC
ΤΟΙCΙΕΡΕΥCΙΝ : ΤΗΑΥΤΗΝΗΜΕΡΑΘΕΑCΑΜΕΝΟC
ΤΙΝΑΕΡΓΑΖΟΜΕΝΟΝΤΩCΑΒΒΑΤΩ ΕΙΠΕΝΑΥΤΩ
ΑΝΘΡΩΠΕ ΕΙΜΕΝΟΙΔΑCΤΙΠΟΙΕΙC
ΜΑΚΑΡΙΟCΕΙΕΙΔΕΜΗΟΙΔΑC ΕΠΙΚΑΤΑΡΑΤΟC
ΚΑΙΠΑΡΑΒΑΤΗCΕΙΤΟΥΝΟΜΟΥ

ΙΗC
ΙΗC
ΔΑΥΕΙΔ

2
quibusnonlicebatmanducaresinonsolis
sacerdotibus eodem die uidens
quendam operante insabbato et dixit illi
homo siquidem scis quod facis
beatus es si autem nescis maledictus
et trabaricator legis

CODEX BEZAE.

PHOTOGRAPH OF ST. LUKE VI., 4, WITH CURIOUS INTERPOLATION. (See p. 32.

Dr. Westcott says " It is evident that it rests on some real incident." It occurs in St. Luke vi., between the fourth and fifth verses. It is in the midst of the Pharisee's disputes with Our Lord about the keeping of the Sabbath. For convenience sake the Latin is photographed underneath the Greek instead of opposite it. The reader can easily follow the Latin on the photograph.

> quibus non licebat manducare si non solis sacerdotibus
> *which it is not lawful to eat but for the priests alone.*

This is the end of v. 4 and then follows the interpolation:

> EODEM DIE VIDENS
> QUENDAM OPERANTEM SABBATO ET DIXIT ILLI
> HOMO SIQUIDEM SCIS QUOD FACIS
> BEATUS ES. SI AUTEM NESCIS MALEDICTUS
> ET TRABARICATOR LEGIS.

> THE SAME DAY SEEING
> A CERTAIN MAN WORKING ON THE SABBATH HE SAID TO HIM
> MAN IF INDEED THOU KNOWEST WHAT THOU ART DOING
> HAPPY ART THOU. BUT IF THOU KNOWEST NOT THOU ART AC-
> CURSED AND A TRANSGRESSOR OF THE LAW.

VI.

All that we have examined up to this date are of uncial type, which, as we have seen, is a mark of their antiquity. Of these Uncials we have altogether about a hundred.

Of the more modern manuscripts, in the cursive

or running hand, there are more than 1500 accessible to scholars. It has been already remarked that it is quite possible for a comparatively modern manuscript to possess a high value, as, for example, suppose a scribe of the fifteenth century had copied in running hand direct from the " Vatican."   For this and other reasons some of our Cursives are very important evidence. There is one, for instance, the " Queen of the Cursives," as it is called, which, for its valuable readings, ranks above many a far older Uncial, and there are four others, quite modern in date (twelfth to fourteenth centuries), which have been shown by Professor Abbott and the late Professor Ferrar, of Trinity College, Dublin,[1] to be transcribed from one and the same ancient manuscript, which was probably little later than our Alexandrian Codex.

If we remember that ten or twelve manuscripts, and these generally modern, are all we have for ascertaining the text of most classical authors, it will help us to understand what an enormous mass of evidence there is available for the purpose of Scripture revision.

[1] " Collation of Four Important Manuscripts," by W. H. Ferrar, F.T.C.D., edited by T. K. Abbott, F.T.C.D. Dublin, 1877.

VII.

The Hebrew manuscripts of the Old Testament need occupy little time. It is rather startling to learn that the earliest Hebrew manuscripts in existence date no earlier than about the tenth century, A. D., *i. e.,* about the time of William the Conqueror! This is a grave disadvantage to the textual criticism of the Old Testament, more especially since the Hebrew alphabet and method of writing have quite changed since the days of the prophets. The lack of early manuscripts here is, however, of less importance than would appear at first sight. As far as we can learn there seems to have been a gradual rough sort of revision of the Palestine manuscripts continually going on almost from the days of Ezra. About a thousand years ago this process of Hebrew Manuscript Revision came to an end, and thus at that early date the Hebrew Old Testament was made as nearly correct as the best scholarship of the Jewish academies could make it, after which the older manuscripts gradually disappeared.*

The existing Hebrew manuscripts, then, though not very old, are of great authority, and all the more so owing to the reverence of Jewish scribes

* For the story of the Hebrew manuscripts, see the author's " The Old Documents and the New Bible."

3

for the Word of God, and the consequent careful-
ness of their transcription. So scrupulous were
they that even if a manifest error were in the copy
they transcribed from, they would not meddle with
it in the text, but would write in the margin what
the true reading should be; if they found one letter larger than another, or a word running beyond
the line, or any other mere irregularity, they
would copy it exactly as it stood. They recorded
how many verses in each book, and the middle
verse of each, and how many verses began with
particular letters, &c., &c. Such exactness, of
course, very much lessened the danger of erro-
neous copying, and makes our Hebrew Scriptures
far more trustworthy than they could otherwise be.

The reason then that there are so few changes
in the Revised Old Testament, as compared with
the New, is that we have probably less need and
certainly less means of making any corrections.[1]
In fact, the chief grounds for undertaking Old
Testament revision are the increased knowledge
of Hebrew and of textual criticism, together with
the changes through natural growth of the English
language itself. We may add also, for their
united evidence is very important, the more thor-

[1] It is no reflection on the Old Testament revisers to suggest
also that they could scarcely avoid being influenced in some
degree by the strong feeling exhibited against the many changes
in the New Testament portion.

ough study in the late years of the Septuagint and the Targums, together with the Vulgate and other ancient versions, to be described in the next chapter.

CHAPTER III.

ANCIENT VERSIONS AND QUOTATIONS.

I.

WE are to examine now our second pile—the
ANCIENT VERSIONS, *i. e.*, the translations of the
Bible into the languages of early Christendom
long before the oldest of our present Greek manuscripts were written.   These were the Bibles used
by men, some of whose parents might easily have
seen the apostles themselves, and therefore it is
evident that, even though only translations, they
must often be of great value in determining the
original text.

There are the old Syriac Scriptures, which were
probably in use about fifty years after the New
Testament was written, a Version representing
very nearly the language of the people among
whom our Lord moved.   Those discolored parchments beside them are Egyptian, Ethiopic, and

Armenian Versions, which would be more useful if our scholars understood these languages better; and the beautiful silver-lettered book, with its leaves of purple parchment, is the Version of Ulfilas, bishop of the fierce Gothic tribes about A. D. 350.[1] Here are the "Old Latin," which, with the Syriac, are the earliest of all our Versions, and the most valuable for the purpose of textual criticism.

But what is this Version piled up in such enormous numbers, far exceeding that of all the others put together, some of its copies, too, ornamented with exquisite beauty?

II.

It is a Version which in these days of the English "Revised Version" should possess special interest for English readers—St. Jerome's Latin Vulgate, the great "Revised Version" of the ancient Western Church. This is its story.

Toward the end of the fourth century, so many errors had crept into the "Old Latin" Versions that the Latin-speaking churches were in danger of losing the pure Scripture of the apostolic days. Just at this crisis, when scholars were keenly feel-

[1] Gibbons says: "He prudently suppressed the four books of Kings, as they might tend to irritate the fierce spirit of the barbarians."

ing the need of a revision, there returned to Rome
from his Bethlehem hermitage one of the greatest
scholars and holiest men of the day, Eusebius
Hieronymus better known to us as St. Jerome,
and his high reputation pointed him out at once
as the man to undertake this important task.
Damasus, bishop of Rome, applied to him for
that purpose, and Jerome undertook the revision,
though he was deeply sensible of the prejudice
which his work would arouse among those who, he
says, " thought that ignorance was holiness." His
revision of the New Testament was completed in
385, and the Old Testament he afterward translated direct from the original Hebrew, a task
which probably no other Christian scholar of the
time would have been capable of. We shall better
understand the value of his work if we remember
that it is almost as old as the earliest of our present Greek manuscripts, and since Jerome of course
used the oldest manuscripts to be had in his day,
his authorities would probably have extended back
to the days of the apostles.

No other work has ever had such an influence
on the history of the Bible. For more than a
thousand years it was the parent of every version
of the Scriptures [1] in Western Europe, and even
now, when the Greek and Hebrew manuscripts are
so easily accessible, the Rhemish and Douay Tes-

[1] See Diagram facing the title-page.

taments are translations direct from the Vulgate, and its influence is quite perceptible even on our own Authorized Version.

III.

How do you think the good people of the fourth century thanked St. Jerome for his wonderful Bible? Remembering the prejudice which our Revised Version excited not many years ago, it is interesting to recall the story how the Revision of the old monk of Bethlehem was received.

It was called revolutionary and heretical; it was pronounced subversive of all faith in Holy Scriptures; it was said to be an impious altering of the Inspired Word of God. In fact, for centuries after, everything was said against it that ignorant bigotry could suggest to bring it into disrepute. The Christians of that day had their old Bible, which they venerated highly and believed to be quite correct, and probably the sound of its sentences was as musical in their ears, who could associate them with the holiest moments of their lives, as that of our beautiful Authorized Version is in ours.

But St. Jerome fought his battle, perhaps with more temper than was necessary,[1] insisting that no

[1] Thus, writing to Marcella, he mentions certain poor creatures (homunculos), who studiously calumniate him for his cor-

amount of sentiment could be a plea for a faulty Bible, and that the most venerable translation must give way if found to disagree with the original text.

It is instructive to us to see how completely the tide had turned at the time of the council of Trent, a thousand years later. Men had then got as attached to the version of St. Jerome as those of the fourth century had been to its predecessors. In fact, they seem almost to have forgotten that it was only a translation. It is the version of the Church, they said, and in her own language; "Why should it yield to Greek and Hebrew manuscripts, which have been for all these hundreds of years in the hands of Jewish unbelievers and Greek schismatics?" Well, how did they act? They decreed in council that the old Vulgate should be regarded as the standard text, and to this day, with all the progress in textual research, the Roman Church has held to that decision.

An amusing exhibition of the feeling at the time is a passage in the preface to the Compluten-

recting words in the Gospels. "I could afford to despise them," he says, "if I stood upon my rights; for a lyre is played in vain to an ass. If they do not like the water from the pure fountain-head, let them drink of the muddy streams;" and again, at the close of the letter, he returns to the attack of those "bipedes asellos" (two-legged donkeys). "Let *them* read, '*Rejoicing in hope, serving the time;*' let *us* read, 'Rejoicing in hope, serving the Lord;' let *them* consider that an accusation should not under any circumstances be received against an elder; let *us* read, 'Against an elder receive not an accusation; but before two or three witnesses,'" &c. (Ep. 28).

sian Polyglot Bible, where the Hebrew and the Greek and the Latin Vulgate were printed in parallel columns side by side, the venerable old Vulgate being in the middle, which the editors with grim humor compared to the position of our Lord between the two thieves at the crucifixion! Of course they did not mean any slight to the original Scriptures, but their prejudice led them to suspect, or to fancy they had a right to suspect, that the Jews and Greeks might have corrupted the manuscript copies.

IV.

This glance at the Ancient Versions will be sufficient for our purpose. There is a large number now accessible to scholars, and every year the study of them is increasing. In passing, I would point to this part of our subject to illustrate the advantage indirectly resulting from the investigation of questions suggested by our New Revision. For here we find that at a time when some sceptical writers would have us believe our New Testament books were scarcely written, they had been translated and copied and re-copied in the languages of early Christendom; commentaries and harmonies of the Gospels had been written; a list of the books had been prepared (of which we have still a portion called the Muratorian Fragment), and they were regarded in all arguments between Christians of the time as referees having divine authority. All this will be seen still more clearly after we have briefly glanced at the third source of information open to revisers:

V.

THE QUOTATIONS IN EARLY CHRISTIAN WRITERS. The quantity of these writings is great, but they have been up to this time very imperfectly examined. In spite of the disadvantages of the quotations being often fragmentary, and sometimes —as will be seen in the examples—made loosely from memory, they are yet of great value in determining the text of ancient Bibles, some of them going back to the days of the original New Testament writings. Let us turn over a few of them at random, taking the earliest in preference.

(a.) Here is the Epistle of Barnabas, which Doctor Tischendorf found bound up with his Sinaitic Manuscript. It was supposed, though without good reason, to have been written by St. Paul's companion; but certainly it is not much later than his date. Notice these expressions: "Beware, therefore, lest it come upon us as it is written, ' There be many called but few chosen;' " again, " Give to him that asketh thee." And farther on he says, " that Christ chose as His apostles men who were sinners, because He came not to call the righteous, but sinners to repentance."

(b.) This next is an Epistle by Clement, one of the early bishops of Rome, whom ancient writers unhesitatingly assert to be the Clement mentioned by St. Paul in Phil. iv. 3. This letter is a very valuable one, and Irenæus, who was bishop of Lyons a little later, says of it, " It was written by Clement, who had seen the blessed apostles and conversed with them, who had the preaching of the blessed apostles still sounding in his ears and their tradition before his eyes." The epistle was addressed to the Church of Corinth, and Dionysius, bishop of Corinth about 170 A. D., bears witness " that it had been wont to be read in his church from ancient times." Here are a few expressions found in it: " Remembering the words of the Lord Jesus which He spake, teaching us gentleness and long-suffering; for He said, ' Be merciful, that ye may obtain mercy; forgive, that it may be forgiven unto you; as ye give it shall be given unto you; as ye judge ye shall be judged; with what measure ye mete, it shall be measured to you.' "

And again, " Remember the words of the Lord Jesus, how He said, ' Woe to the man by whom offences come; it were better for him that he had

not been born than that he should offend one of
My elect.   It were better for him that a millstone
should be tied about his neck, and that he should
be drowned in the depths of the sea, than that he
should offend one of My little ones.' ''

(*c.*) Of about the same date is this book, the
Shepherd of Hermas, by some conjectured to be
the Hermas of Rom. xvi. 14.   Here we have reference to the confessing and denying of Christ, the
parable of the seed sown, the expression, " He
that putteth away his wife and marrieth another,
committeth adultery," &c., &c.

(*d.*) St. Ignatius became bishop of Antioch
about forty years after the Ascension.   Here are
a few quotations from him: " Christ was bap-
tized of John, that all righteousness might be fulfilled in Him."   " Be ye wise as serpents in all
things, and harmless as a dove."   " The Spirit is
from God, for it knows whence it cometh and
whither it goeth."

(*e.*) The martyr Polycarp was a disciple of St.
John, and is thus spoken of by Irenæus, bishop of
Lyons, who in his youth had seen him: " I can
tell the place in which the blessed Polycarp sat and
taught, and his going out and coming in, and the
manner of his life, and how he related his conver-
sations with John and others who had seen the
Lord, all which Polycarp related agreeably to the
Scriptures."   Of this old martyr we have an

epistle remaining, and though it is a very short one, it contains nearly forty clear allusions to the New Testament books, some of which are valuable for critical purposes.

(*f.*) Those old parchments lying beside Polycarp's Epistle, are the "Apologies," by Justin Martyr, and his "Dialogue with Trypho," written about the year 150. They contain very interesting quotations, though unfortunately they seem often quoted from memory, and therefore lose much of their value. This is only what we might expect. "When we think it strange," says Dr. Salmon,[1] "that an ancient father of Justin's date should not quote with perfect accuracy, we forget that in those days, when manuscripts were scarce and concordances did not exist, the process of finding a passage in a manuscript (written possibly with no spaces between the words) was not performed with quite as much ease as an English clergyman writing his sermon, with a Bible and Concordance by his side, can turn up any text he wishes to refer to, and yet we should be sorry to vouch for the verbal accuracy of all the Scripture citations we hear in sermons at the present day."

The following are a few of Justin's quotations: " I gave you power to tread on serpents and scorpions, and venomous beasts, and on all the power

---

[1] "Introd. New Testament," p. 82.

of the enemy." "Give to him that asketh, and from him that would borrow turn not away; for if ye lend to them of whom ye hope to receive, what new thing do ye? Even the publicans do this. Lay not up for yourselves treasures upon earth, where moth and rust doth corrupt, and where robbers break through; but lay up for yourselves treasure in heaven, where neither moth nor rust doth corrupt." For what is a man profited if he shall gain the whole world and lose his own soul, or what shall a man give in exchange for it?" And again, "Be ye kind and merciful, as your Father also is kind and merciful, and maketh His sun to rise on sinners, and the righteous and the wicked. Take no thought what ye shall eat or what ye shall put on; are ye not better than the birds and the beasts? and God feedeth them. Take no thought, therefore, what ye shall eat or what ye shall put on, for your heavenly Father knoweth that ye have need of these things. But seek ye the kingdom of heaven, and all these things shall be added unto you. For where his treasure is, there is the mind of man."

On account of the double object in view, I have selected only writers of the second century to illustrate the use of the "Quotations." More important for purposes of criticism, though later in date, are those thick manuscripts further on, the works of Origen and Clement of Alexandria early in the third century, and in the fourth Basil, and Augustine, and Jerome the great reviser, and many others, whose writings in large quantity are available for criticism of the Bible.

CHAPTER IV.

EARLY ENGLISH VERSIONS.

THUS we have seen the form in which the Scriptures existed in the age soon after that of the apostles, and found the threefold line of evidence available at the present day for the purpose of Bible Revision—(1.) Greek and Hebrew manuscripts; (2.) Ancient Versions; and (3.) Quotations from the then existing Scriptures in the works of early Christian writers.

And now that we are to trace the connection of these with our present English Bible, it becomes necessary for our purpose to ask, with the triple pile of parchments before us, how much of this material was accessible a thousand years ago, when the history of our English Bible begins. For it is evident that the value of a Scripture version at any period depends on the value of the old manuscript material accessible, and the ability of the men of that day to use it.

For answer we take from the centre pile those

few faded worn-looking copies, portions of the
Vulgate and older Latin versions, and place them
on the one side.[1]   Those are the Scriptures which
have come down to us from the monasteries of
ancient England, and as we compare side by side
this handful of old parchments with the great
mass of writings from which it has been drawn,
we are comparing together the sources of the
earliest and latest English Versions—of the
Anglo-Saxon Scriptures of a thousand years since,
and the Revised Bible which is in our hands to-
day.[2] The growth of the English Bible, which
took place in the meantime, we are now briefly to
trace.[3]

[1] There were also many works of the early Christian Fathers,
but as no one then thought of using them for purposes of textual
criticism, we need not take them into account.

[2] On page facing the title I have tried to show by a diagram
the gradual increase in the sources of our English Bible.

[3] Here comes a temptation to an Irish writer. Is he bound to
start from the eighth century, when the earliest known translations from these manuscripts were made? May he not go back
a little further, and let rise the historic memories called up by
those manuscripts themselves? May he not indulge a little in
the " Irish pride of better days " (the only source of pride to
poor Ireland in the present), and picture the noble libraries of
Durrow and Armagh, to which England probably owes her
earliest Scriptures—when St. Columb carried his manuscripts to
lonely Iona in the days of the glory of the Irish Church, when
Ireland was the light of the Western World, and Irishmen went
forth from the " Island of Saints " to evangelize the heathen
English?

At any rate it seems worth spending a few sentences to point
out that not from Rome, but from the ancient Irish Church, did
England chiefly derive her Christianity, and probably her
earliest Scriptures. What seems best remembered in connection
with the question, is the famous scene of Gregory in the slave-
market at Rome, admiring the beautiful English children—" not

4

I.

Though England had no complete Bible before Wycliffe's days, attempts were made from very early times to present the Scriptures in the language of the people, and the story of these ancient translations from the Latin manuscripts before us, forms certainly one of the most interesting though not most important portions of the history of the English Bible.

It is now 1200 years since, on a winter night, a poor Saxon cowherd lay asleep in a stable of the famous Abbey of Whitby. Grieved and dispirited, he had come in from the feast where his masters,

Angles, but angels," said he, "if they were only Christians "—and the consequent sending of the Abbot Augustine to England with a band of Christian missionaries. It needs to be pointed out that, according to our best historians, this Roman mission soon lost its early ardor, penetrating little further than Kent, where it originally landed, and that the conversion of England, which had become completely pagan under Saxon rule, was for the most part left to the missionaries of the Irish Church. From St. Columb's monastery at Iona the Irish preachers came, and travelled over the greater part of the country. Aidan, their leader, went through the wilds of Yorkshire and Northumbria with King Oswald as his interpreter, a former student of Iona —while Chad and Boisil led their little bands of missionaries through the centre of the heathen land, returning at stated periods to Lindisfarne, where Aidan had fixed his episcopal see. And not England only owes a debt to the Irish Church. As far off as the Apennines and the Alps the traces of her enthusiastic missionaries are found, and "for a time it seemed as if the course of the world's history was to be changed, as if the older Celtic race, that Roman and German had swept before them, had turned to the moral conquest of their conquerors, as if Celtic and not Latin Christianity was to mould the destinies of the churches of the West." (*Green, History of the English People.*)

and some even of his companions, during the amusements of the night, had engaged in the easy, alliterative rhyming of those simple early days. But Cædmon could make no song,[1] and his soul was very sad. Suddenly, as he lay, it seemed to him that a heavenly glory lighted up his stable, and in the midst of the glory One appeared who had been cradled in a manger six hundred years before.

"Sing, Cædmon," He said, "sing some song to me."

"I cannot sing," was the sorrowful reply, "for this cause it is that I came hither."

"Yet," said He who stood before him, "yet shalt thou sing to me."

"What shall I sing?"

"The beginning of created things."

And as he listened, a divine power seemed to come on him, and words that he had never heard before rose up before his mind.[2] And so the

---

[1] Being at the feast, when all agreed for glee sake to sing in turn, he no sooner saw the harp come toward him, than he rose from the board and returned homeward."—*Account of Cædmon in Bede's Eccl. Hist.*

[2] The words that came to the sleeper's mind are recorded by King Alfred. They begin:

> "Now must we praise
> the grandeur of Heaven's kingdom;
> the Creator's might,
> and his mind's thought;
> glorious father of men,
> The Lord the Eternal,
> who formed the beginning," &c., &c.

vision passed away. But the power remained with Cædmon, and in the morning the Saxon cowherd went forth from the cattle-stalls transformed into a mighty poet!

Hilda the abbess heard the wondrous tale, and from one of those Latin manuscripts she translated to him a story of the Scriptures. Next day it was reproduced in a beautiful poem, followed by another and another as the spirit of the poet grew powerful within him. Entranced, the abbess and the brethren heard, and they acknowledged the " grace that had been conferred on him by the Lord." They bade him lay aside his secular habit and enter the monastic life, and from that day forward the Whitby cowherd devoted himself with enthusiasm to the task that had been set him in the vision. " Others after him strove to compose religious poems, but none could vie with him, for he learned not the art of poetry from men, neither of men, but of God." In earnest passionate words, which yet remain, he sung for the simple people " of the creation of the world, of the origin of man, and of all the history of Israel; of the Incarnation, and Passion, and Resurrection of Christ, and His Ascension; of the terror of future judgment, the horror of hell pains, and the joys of the kingdom of heaven." [1]

[1] Some account of Cædmon from Bede's Eccl. Hist., translated into Anglo-Saxon by King Alfred."—*Published by the Society of Antiquaries, London.*

Though his work has of course no right to rank among Bible translations, being merely an attempt to sing for the ignorant people the substance of the inspired story, yet we venture to give a brief extract, translated into modern English, telling of the appearance of Christ to His disciples after the resurrection:

> " What time the Lord God
> from death arose
> so strongly was no
> Satan armed
> though he were with iron
> all girt round
> that might that great
> force resist;
> for he went forth
> the Lord of angels,
> in the strong city,
> and bade fetch
> angels all bright
> and even bade say
> to Simon Peter
> that he might on Galilee
> behold God
> eternal and firm,
> as he ere did.
> Then as I understand, went
> the disciples together
> all to Galilee,
> inspired by the Spirit,
> The holy Son of God,
> whom they saw

were the Lord's son.
Then over against the disciples stood
the Lord Eternal,
God in Galilee,
so that the disciples
thither all ran
Where the eternal was,
fell on the earth,
and at his feet bowed,
thanking the Lord
that thus it befell
that they should behold
the creator of angels.
Then forthwith spake
Simon Peter and said,
Art thou thus, Lord,
with power gifted?
We saw thee
at one time when
they laid thee
in loathsome bondage,
the heathen with their hands.
That they may rue
when they their end
shall behold hereafter.

. . . .

He on the tree ascended
and shed his blood,
God on the cross
through his Spirit's power.
Wherefore we should
at all times
give to the Lord thanks
in deeds and works

for that he us from thraldom
led home
up to Heaven,
where we may share
the greatness of God." [1]

II.

About the time of Cædmon's death, early in the eighth century, the learned Eadhelm, bishop of Sherborne, was working in Glastonbury Abbey translating the Psalms of David into Anglo-Saxon, and at his request, it is said, Egbert, bishop of Holy Island, completed about the same time a version of the Gospels, of which a copy is still preserved in the British Museum.

III.

But the names of Eadhelm and Egbert are overshadowed by that of a contemporary far greater than either.

It was a calm peaceful evening in the spring of 735—the evening of Ascension Day—and in his quiet cell in the monastery of Jarrow an aged monk lay dying. With labored utterance he tried to dictate to his scribe, while a group of fair-haired Saxon youths stood sorrowfully by, with tears beseeching their " dear master " to rest.

[1] Thorpe's " Cædmon's Paraphrase."—*Society of Antiquaries, London,* 1832.

That dying monk was the most famous scholar of his day in Western Europe. Through him Jarrow-on-the-Tyne had become the great centre of literature and science, hundreds of eager students crowding yearly to its halls to learn of the famous Bæda. He was deeply versed in the literature of Greece and Rome—he had written on medicine, and astronomy, and rhetoric, and most of the other known sciences of the time—his " Ecclesiastical History " is still the chief source of our knowledge of ancient England;—but none of his studies were to him equal to the study of religion, none of his books of the same importance as his commentaries and sermons on Scripture. Even then as he lay on his deathbed he was feebly dictating to his scribe a translation of St. John's Gospel. " I don't want my boys to read a lie," he said, " or to work to no purpose after I am gone."

And those " boys " seem to have dearly loved the gentle old man. An epistle has come down to us from his disciple Cuthbert to a " fellow reader " Cuthwin, telling of what had happened this Ascension Day. " Our father and master, whom God loved," he says, " had translated the Gospel of St. John as far as ' what are these among so many,' when the day came before Our Lord's Ascension.

" He began then to suffer much in his breath,

and a swelling came in his feet, but he went on dictating to his scribe. 'Go on quickly,' he said, 'I know not how long I shall hold out, or how soon my Master will call me hence.'

"All night long he lay awake in thanksgiving, and when the Ascension Day dawned, he commanded us to write with all speed what he had begun."

Thus the letter goes on affectionately, describing the working and resting right through the day till the evening came, and then, with the setting sun gilding the windows of his cell, the old man lay feebly dictating the closing words.

"There remains but one chapter, master," said the anxious scribe, "but it seems very hard for you to speak."

"Nay, it is easy," Bede replied; "take up thy pen and write quickly."

Amid blinding tears the young scribe wrote on. "And now, father," said he, as he eagerly caught the last words from his quivering lips, "only one sentence remains." Bede dictated it.

"It is finished, master!" cried the youth, raising his head as the last word was written.

"Ay, it is finished!" echoed the dying saint; "lift me up, place me at that window of my cell where I have so often prayed to God. Now glory be to the Father, and to the Son, and to the Holy

Ghost!" and with these words the beautiful spirit passed to the presence of the Eternal Trinity.

IV.

Our next translator is no less a person than King Alfred the Great, whose patriotic wish has been so often quoted, "that all the freeborn youth of his kingdom should employ themselves on nothing till they could first read well the English Scripture." [1]

A striking monument of his zeal for the Bible remains in the beginning of his Laws of England. The document is headed "Alfred's Dooms," and begins thus: "The dooms which the Almighty Himself spake to Moses, and gave him to keep, and after our Saviour Christ came to earth, He said He came not to break or forbid, but to keep them." And then follow the Ten Commandments, in the forcible simple Anglo-Saxon terms, the first part of the ancient laws of England:

Drihten wæs sprecende thæs word to Moyse and thus cwæth:

Ic eam Drihten thy God. Ic the sit gelædde of Aegypta londe and of heora theowdome.

The Lord was speaking these words to Moses and thus said:

I am the Lord thy God. I led thee out of the land of Egypt and its thralldom.

[1] At least so it is quoted, though the last words "Englisc ge-writ arædan" quite as probably mean "to read English *writing.*" See Eadie's Bibl. Hist., i. 13.

Ne lufa thu othre fremde godas ofer me.

* * * * *

Ara thinum fæder and thinre meder tha the Drihten sealde the, that thu sy thy leng libbende on eorthan.

Ne slea thu.

Ne stala thu.

Ne lige thu dearnunga.

Ne sæge thu lease gewitnesse with thinum nehstan.

Ne wilna thu thines nehstan yifes mid unrihte.

Ne wyrc thu the gyldene godas ohthe seolfrene.

Love thou not other strange gods over me.

* * * * *

Honor thy father and thy mother whom the Lord gave thee, that thou be long living on earth.

Slay not thou.

Steal not thou.

Commit not thou adultery.

Say not thou false witness against thy neighbor.

Desire not thou thy neighbor's inheritance with unright.

Work not thou the golden gods or silvern.

Here is the Lord's Prayer of King Alfred's time, and side by side with it the Lord's Prayer in early English three hundred years afterward:

Uren Fader dhis art in heofnas,

Sic gehalged dhin noma,

To cymedh dhin ric,

Sic dhin uuilla sue is in heofnas and in eardho,

Vren hlaf ofer uuirthe sel vs to daeg,

And forgef us scylda urna,

Sue uue forgefan sculdgun vrum,

And no inleadh vridk in costnung al gefrig vrich from ifle.

Fader oure that art in heve,

I-halgeed be thi nome,

I-cume thi kinereiche,

Y-worthe thi wylle also is in hevene so be on erthe,

Our iche-days-bred gif us to-day,

And forgif us oure gultes,

Also we forgifet oure gultare,

And ne led ows nowth into fondyngge, Auth ales ows of harme,

So be hit.

Alfred also engaged in a translation of the Psalms, which, with the Gospels, seemed the favorite Scriptures of the people; but, unlike his great predecessor, Bede, he died before his task was finished.

V.

Archbishop Aelfric, and a few other translattors, appear about the close of the tenth century, but there is no need of describing their works in detail. As far as we can judge from the existing manuscripts, most of these early Bible translations were intended for reading in the churches to the people, and their simple expressive terms made them very easily understood. For example, a centurion was a " hundred-man," a disciple a " leorning cnight," or " learning youth; " " the man with the dropsy," is translated as " the water-seocman," the Sabbath as " the reste daeg " (rest day), and the woman who put her mites in the treasury, is said to have cast them into the " goldhoard." [1]

On the opposite page is a photograph of Archbishop Aelfric's Anglo-Saxon Bible. It is taken from a beautiful copy in the Cottonian Library. It contains many curious miniatures as for example the Creation of Eve who is represented as being

[1] See Forshall and Madden's Anglo-Saxon Gospels.

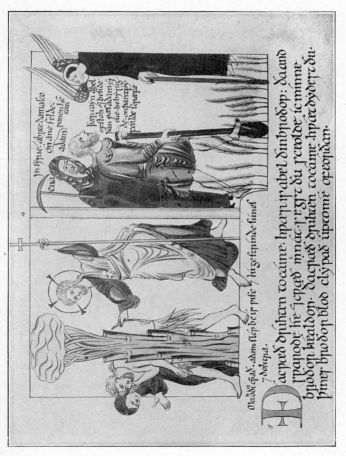

ARCHBISHOP AELFRIC'S ANGLO-SAXON BIBLE, 11TH CENTURY.

drawn out of an opening amongst Adam's ribs. The miniature which we reproduce represents the expulsion of Adam and Eve from Paradise and their being taught by an angel to till the ground. Below it is photographed a verse from a later page (Gen. iv. 9, 10). It is interesting to notice in this passage that almost every word of its Anglo-Saxon is still represented in our present English:

Tha   cwæth Drihten to Caine hwaer is Abel
Then quoth   the Lord to   Cain where is   Abel

thin brothor: tha andswarode he & cwæth
thy   brother: then   answered   he &   quoth

is nat,   segst thu sceolde is minne brothor &c.
I know not, sayest thou should I   my   brother &c.

The following is a New Testament specimen from Forshall and Madden's Anglo-Saxon Gospels.

St. Matt. vii. 26, 27.

And aelc thaera the gehyrath thas mine word
And each of them that ge-heareth these mine words

and tha ne wyrcth   se bith gelic thon
and that not worketh (them) he beeth ge-like that

dysigan   man tha getimbrode hys hus ofer
foolish (dizzy) man that   timbered   his house over

sand-ceosel.   Tha rinde hyt and thaer comun flod
sand-gravel.   Then rained it and there   come flood

and bleowun windas and ahruron on thon hus,
and   blew   winds and rushed   on   that house,

and that hus feoll and hys hryre wæes mycel.
and that house fell and his   fall   was   mickle.

CHAPTER V.

WYCLIFFE'S VERSION.

WE pass over six hundred silent years.

After the early Anglo-Saxon versions comes a
long pause in the history of Bible translation.
Amid the disturbance resulting from the Danish
invasion there was little time for thinking of translations and manuscripts; and before the land had
fully regained its quiet the fatal battle of Hastings
had been fought, and England lay helpless at the
feet of the Normans. The higher Saxon clergy
were replaced by the priests of Normandy, who
had little sympathy with the people over whom
they were placed, and the Saxon manuscripts were
contemptuously flung aside as relics of a rude bar-
barism. The contempt shown to the language of
the defeated race quite destroyed the impulse to
English translation, and the Norman clergy had
no sympathy with the desire for spreading the

knowledge of the Scriptures among the people, so that for centuries those Scriptures remained in England a " spring shut up, a fountain sealed."

Yet this time must not be considered altogether lost, for during those centuries England was becoming fitted for an English Bible. The future language of the nation was being formed; the Saxon and Norman French were struggling side by side; gradually the old Saxon grew unintelligible to the people; gradually the French became a foreign tongue, and with the fusion of the two races a language grew up which was the language of United England.[1]

[1] "In tracing the history of the change from Anglo-Saxon to modern English it is impossible to assign any precise dates by which we can mark the origin of this change, or the principal epochs of its progress, or its completion. This necessarily results from the very gradual nature of the change itself; we might as well ask at what moment a child becomes a youth, or a youth a man; or when the plant becomes a tree. So gradual was the change, that, to adopt the language of Hallam, ' When we compare the earliest English of the thirteenth century with the Anglo-Saxon of the twelfth, it seems hard to pronounce why it should pass for a separate language rather than a modification and simplification of the former.' Still, for the sake of convenience, we may fix on certain dates somewhere about which the change commenced or was effected. About 1150, or a little less than a century after the Conquest, may be dated the decline of pure Saxon; about 1250, or a century later, the commencement of English. During the intervening century the language has been called by many of our writers semi-Saxon."—*H. Rogers in Edinburgh Review, Oct.,* 1850.

It was toward the end of the fourteenth century that English began to be the language of literature. " Sir John Mandeville's Travels," one of the earliest English books, appeared in 1356, and Chaucer wrote toward the close of the century; therefore Wycliffe's Bible in 1383 was about as early as a version could be which was to retain its place among the English people.

II.

Passing, then, from the quiet deathbeds of Alfred and Bede, we transfer ourselves to the great hall of the Blackfriars' Monastery, London, on a day in May, 1378, amid purple robes and gowns of satin and damask, amid monks and abbots, and bishops and doctors of the Church, assembled for the trial of John Wycliffe, the parish priest of Lutterworth.

The great hall, crowded to its heavy oaken doors, witnesses to the interest that is centred in the trial, and all eyes are fixed on the pale stern old man who stands before the dais silently facing his judges. He is quite alone, and his thoughts go back, with some bitterness, to his previous trial, when the people crowded the doors shouting for their favourite, and John of Gaunt and the Lord Marshal of England were standing by his side. He has learned since then not to put his trust in princes. The power of his enemies has grown rapidly, even the young King has been won over to their cause, and patrons and friends have drawn back from the side of him whom the Church has resolved to crush.

The judges have taken their seats, and the accused stands awaiting the charges to be read, when suddenly there is a quick cry of terror. A

strange rumbling sound fills the air, and the walls
of the judgment-hall are trembling to their base
—the monastery and the city of London are being
shaken by an earthquake! Friar and prelate grow
pale with superstitious awe. Twice already has
the arraignment of Wycliffe been strangely interrupted.   Are the elements in league with this
troubler of the Church? Shall they give up the
trial?

"No!" thunders Archbishop Courtenay, rising
in his place, "We will not give up the trial. This
earthquake but portends the purging of the kingdom; for as there are in the bowels of the earth
noxious vapors which only by a violent earthquake
can be purged away, so are there evils brought
by such men upon this land which only by a very
earthquake can ever be removed. Let the trial go
forward!"

III.

We pause in this place to try to understand the
position of the Church of England at this time,
and the fact that we have here under censure by
that Church the man who was giving to England
her first complete Bible.

It was a critical time in the history of the
English Church. We have evidence of much simple godliness, of real religion, and of many faith-

ful priests all over the land quietly bringing the blessings of religion to their flocks. But it was in the main an age of ignorance and superstition and of worldly ambition in the high places of the Church. Chaucer and other writers of the time give us graphic pictures of its mingled good and evil. The clergy were in the main poorly educated. The Friars who at their first coming had been such a power for good with their ideals of holiness and voluntary poverty, and the popular enthusiasm roused by their preaching, had now in the course of time become degraded into idle vagrants and imposters extorting money by the selling of pardons and relics, " as if," to quote the words of an old writer, " God had given His sheep not to be pastured but to be shaven and shorn." The Roman See, too, was encroaching more and more on the liberties of the Church of England and rousing the ancient spirit of the Barons' Charter at Runnymede, " Ecclesia Anglicana libera sit." " The Church of England must be free." A hostile spirit was growing in the nation a spirit which might easily turn from hostility to the Papacy to hostility toward religion itself.

The times were critical and those who could discern the signs of the times must have seen now that things could not go on much longer as they were. For education was rapidly increasing, several new colleges having been founded in Oxford during Wycliffe's lifetime. A strong spirit of independence, too, was rising among the people—already Edward III. and his Parliament had indignantly refused the Pope's demand for the annual tribute to be sent to Rome. It was evident that a crisis was near. And, as if to hasten the crisis, the famous schism of the Papacy had placed two Popes at the head of the Church, and all Christendom was scandalized by the sight of the rival "vicars of Jesus Christ" anathematizing each other from Rome and Avignon, raising armies and slaughtering helpless women and children, each for the aggrandizement of himself.

IV.

Chief amongst the leaders of the patriotic agitation against Roman aggression was John Wycliffe. He was a famous scholar and leader of thought in university circles as well as amongst the populace, and a beautiful life of devotion and self-sacrifice consecrated his great learning. He had a powerful following, John of Gaunt, the Duke of Lancaster, being one of his staunch supporters. And he used his great influence not only against external aggressions from the Papacy but also against internal corruptions in the Church of England itself. Looking back now on certain periods of his career one is inclined to wonder that the English Reformation of 200 years later did not come in Wycliffe's day.

His sermons were a great power. His vigorous pamphlets were sent in all directions. He had organized his band of " poor priests," somewhat on the model of the original friars, to spread the teaching of the Gospel through the land. But immeasurably above all other influences was the splendid project of giving to his Church and nation the first complete Bible in the language of the people. Wycliffe was a most devoted student of Scripture. It was his constant companion, his absolute standard of appeal, and he shows the most intimate acquaintance with its text. In one single volume he has seven hundred quotations from Scripture, and it was his contemporaries' recognition of his reverence for it that gained for him the title of the Evangelical Doctor. Naturally such a man would feel that at such a time the firmest charter of the Church would be the open Bible in her children's hands; the best exposure of the Papal policy, the exhibiting to the people the beautiful self-forgetting life of Jesus Christ as recorded in the Gospels. " The Sacred Scriptures," he said, " are the property of the people, and one which no one should be allowed to wrest from them. . . . Christ and His apostles converted the world by making known the Scriptures to men in a form familiar to them, . . . and I

pray with all my heart that through doing the
things contained in this book we may all together
come to the everlasting life." This Bible translation he placed far the first in importance of all his
attempts to reform the English Church, and he
pursued his object with a vigor and against an
opposition that reminds one of the old monk of
Bethlehem and his Bible a thousand years before.

V.

And yet it must be frankly acknowledged that
John Wycliffe was not the man to accomplish a
reform in the Church of England. He had great
qualities, but he had the defects of his great qualities. He was a born fighter and England sorely
needed such at the time. But like many another
great fighter he was rather destructive than con-
structive. He was better at attacking faults than
at laying down a practical scheme of Church
reform such as would appeal to sensible men.

It would be utterly unfair to blame him for the
wild teaching of his followers after his death. But
he was an incautious teacher. And as he grew
older opposition tended to make him extreme and
one-sided. He became almost an anti-clerical. If
he had his way he would have made a clean sweep
of much of the ministerial forms and ancient

usages of the Church. From attacking the faults
of certain bishops he went on to attack the insti-
tution of episcopacy itself. He laid little stress
on Baptism, though he did splendid work in vindi-
cating the position of Holy Communion. He
spoke slightingly of the accustomed ritual of the
Church service, and some of his writings would
almost suggest that his ideal of a church would be
just a set of wandering preachers of the Gospel,
and not necessarily very well educated preachers
either, for in his later years he spoke slightingly
even of learning in the clergy. " The Apostles,"
he says, " had no college degrees." However
deeply we sympathize with Wycliffe's ideals and
self-devotion yet looking back now, one sees the
grave probability that a Reformation carried out
on his lines would have been dangerous to the continuity of the Church itself.

It is necessary to think of this if we would judge
quite fairly the opposition of the leading English
Churchmen to Wycliffe and his Bible. It is quite
true that many of them were unspiritual men. It
is quite true too that there was a strong prejudice
against the innovation of spreading the Bible
freely amongst the " ignorant laity." One of the
charges against Wycliffe was that he had made the
Bible common and more open to laymen and even
to women (!) than it was wont to be to clergy
well learned and of good understanding, so that

the pearl of the Gospel is trodden under foot of swine."

But it is only fair to say that in this case there was also a strong suspicion of the translator and fear of his theological ideas manifesting itself in his translation.   We can see now that this suspicion was unfounded.   But the suspicion was there.   Perhaps a wiser and more tactful reformer who could win the confidence of his brother Churchmen might have made very different the story of the first English Bible.   But indomitable courage was the chief thing needed just then and it would have been a very unusual type of man who, fighting sternly the dark abuses of that day, could have accurately kept his balance.

VI.

The result of the trial at Blackfriars was that after three days' deliberation Wycliffe's teaching was condemned and at a subsequent meeting he himself was excommunicated.   But he was allowed to return to his quiet parsonage at Lutterworth, for his opponents did not care to proceed to extremities and there with his pile of old Latin manuscripts and commentaries he laboured on at finishing the great work of his life till the whole Bible was translated into the " modir tonge," and England received for the first time in her history a complete version of the Scriptures [1] in the language of the people.

And scarce was his task well finished when, like his great predecessor Bede, the brave old priest laid down his life. He himself had expected that a violent death would have finished his course. His enemies were many and powerful; the primate, the king, and the Pope were against him, with the friars, whom he had so often and so fiercely defied; [2] so that his destruction seemed but

[1] This honour has by some been denied to Wycliffe, chiefly on the authority of Sir Thomas More. "Ye schall understande," he says, "that ye great arch heretike John Wycliffe, whereas ye Holy Bible was long before his dayes by vertuous and well lerned men translated into ye Englische tong and by good and godly people with devotion and soberness well and reverently read, tooke upon him of malicious purpose to translate it anew. In whiche translacioun he purposely corrupted ye Holy Text, maliciously planting therein such wordes as might in ye reders' eres serve to the profe of such heresies as he was aboute to sowe. . . . Myself haue seen and can shew you Bibles fayre and olde, written in Englische, which have been known and seen by ye bischop of ye dyoces and left in lemen's hands and women's."

However, he gives us no means of testing his statement, and the fullest investigation gives no trace of anything but separate fragments of Scripture before Wycliffe's time. Perhaps Sir Thomas More had seen some of Wycliffe's own copies, and mistook them for the work of another and earlier writer, or more probably the statement was made hastily and without proper foundation. A few partial translations had been accomplished in the century before Wycliffe by Scorham, Rolle of Hampole, and others, but they were little known. Wycliffe's great complaint is that there is no English translation of the Scriptures.

[2] The scene has frequently been described of the friars pressing round what seemed the deathbed of their old assailant, adjuring him to recant and receive their absolution, and the stern old man raising himself suddenly to startle them with his fierce prophetic cry, "I shall not die, but live to declare again the evil deeds of the friars!"

a mere question of time.   But while his friends were anxiously anticipating the worst, the old man " was not, for God took him."

It was the close of the Old Year, the last Sunday of 1384, and his little flock at Lutterworth were kneeling in hushed reverence before the altar, when suddenly, at the time of the elevation of the Sacrament, he fell to the ground in a violent fit of the palsy, and never spoke again until his death on the last day of the year.

In him England lost one of her best and greatest sons, a patriot sternly resenting all dishonour to his country, a reformer who ventured his life for the purity of the Church and the freedom of the Bible—an earnest, faithful " parsoun of a toune " standing out conspicuously among the clergy of the time,

> " For Christè's lore and his apostles twelve
> He taughte—and first he folwede it himselve." [1]

A horrible comment on the intolerant spirit of the time is this extract from one of the monkish writers of the time describing his death:—" On the feast of the passion of St. Thomas of Canterbury, John Wycliffe, the organ of the devil, the enemy of the Church, the idol of heretics, the

---

[1] Chaucer's *Prologue*, 527. The whole of that exquisite description of the " parsoun " is supposed to refer to Wycliffe, whose teaching the poet had warmly embraced.

image of hypocrites, the restorer of schism, the storehouse of lies, the sink of flattery, being struck by the horrible judgment of God, was seized with the palsy throughout his whole body, and that mouth which was to have spoken huge things against God and His saints, and holy Church, was miserably drawn aside, and afforded a frightful spectacle to beholders; his tongue was speechless and his head shook, showing plainly that the curse which God had thundered forth against Cain was also inflicted on him."

Some time after his death a petition was presented to the Pope, which to his honour he rejected, praying him to order Wycliffe's body to be taken out of consecrated ground and buried in a dung-hill. But forty years after, by a decreè of the Council of Constance, the old Reformer's bones were dug up and burned, and the ashes flung into the little river Swift, which " runneth hard by his church at Lutterworth." And so, in the oft-quoted words of old Fuller, " as the Swift bare them into the Severn, and the Severn into the narrow seas, and they again into the ocean, thus the ashes of Wycliffe is an emblem of his teaching, which is now dispersed over all the world."

VII.

But it is with his Bible translation that we are specially concerned. As far as we can learn, the whole Bible was not translated by the Reformer. About half the Old Testament is ascribed to Nicholas de Hereford,[1] one of the Oxford leaders of the Lollards, the remainder, with the whole of the New Testament, being done by Wycliffe himself. About eight years after its completion the whole was revised by Richard Purvey, his curate and intimate friend, whose manuscript is still in the library of Trinity College, Dublin. Purvey's preface is a most interesting old document, and shows not only that he was deeply in earnest about his work, but that he thoroughly understood the intellectual and moral conditions necessary for its success.

" A simpel creature," he says, " hath translated

---

[1] He appears to have stopped abruptly in the middle of the verse (Baruch iii. 20), probably at the time of his seizure for heresy. Here is a specimen of his translation, Psalm xxiii. :—
" The Lord gouerneth me and no thing to me shal lacke; in the place of leswe where he me ful sette. Ouer watir of fulfilling he nurshide me; my soule he conuertide. He broghte down upon me the sties of rightwiseness; for his name. For whi and if I shal go in the myddel of the shadewe of deth; I shal not dreden euelis, for thou art with me. Thi yerde and thi staf; the han confortid me. Thou hast maad redi in thi sighte a bord; aghen them that trublyn me. Thou hast myche fatted in oile myn hed and my chalis makende ful drunken, hou right cler it is. And thi mercy shall vnderfolewe me; alle the dayis of my lif. And that I dwelle in the hous of the Lord in to the lengthe of dayis."

the Scripture out of Latin into Englische. First, this simpel creature had much travayle with divers fellows and helpers to gather many old Bibles and other doctors and glosses to make one Latin Bible some deal true and then to study it anew the texte and any other help he might get, especially Lyra on the Old Testament, which helped him much with this work. The third time to counsel with olde grammarians and divines of hard words and hard sentences how they might best be understood and translated, the fourth time to translate as clearly as he could to the sense, and to have many good fellows and cunnyng at the correcting of the translacioun. . . . A translator hath great nede to studie well the sense both before and after, and then also he hath nede to live a clene life and be full devout in preiers, and have not his wit occupied about worldli things that the Holy Spyrit author of all wisdom and cunnynge and truthe dresse him for his work and suffer him not to err." And he concludes with the prayer, " God grant to us all grace to ken well and to kepe well Holie Writ, and to suffer joiefulli some paine for it at the laste."

Like all the earlier English translations, Wycliffe's Bible was only a translation of a translation. It was based on the Latin Vulgate of St. Jerome; and this is the great defect in his work, as compared with the versions that followed. He was

not capable of consulting the original Greek and
Hebrew even if he had access to them—in fact,
there was probably no man in England at the time
capable of doing so; and therefore, though he
represents the Latin faithfully and well, the Version had grown corrupted in the course of trans-
mission and he of course handed on its errors as
faithfully as its perfections. But, such as it is, it
is a fine specimen of fourteenth century English.
He translated not for scholars nor for nobles, but
for the plain people, and his style was such as
suited those for whom he wrote—plain, vigorous,
homely, and yet with all its homeliness full of a
solemn grace and dignity, which made men feel
that they were reading no ordinary book. He
uses many striking expressions, such as 2 Tim.
ii. 4, "No man holding knighthood to God,
wlappith himself with worldli nedes;" and many
of the best-known phrases in our present Bible
originated with him, *e. g.*, "the beame and the
mote," "the depe thingis of God," "strait is the
gate and narewe is the waye," "no but a man
schall be born againe," "the cuppe of blessing
which we blessen," &c., &c.

On the opposite page we give a specimen from
Wycliffe's Gospels, and it will be an interesting
illustration of the growth of our language to compare it, on the one hand, with the specimens 400
years earlier given in the previous chapter, and

on the other with the present Revised Version, which is later in date by 500 years. The resemblance to the latter will be still more marked if the sound only is followed, disregarding the spelling.

MATT. III. 1–6.—**In thilke dayes came Joon Baptist prechynge in the desert of Jude, saying, Do ye penaunce: for the kyngdom of heuens shall neigh. Forsothe this is he of whom it is said by Ysaye the prophete, A voice of a crynge in desert, Make ye redy the wayes of the Lord, make ye rightful the pathes of hym. Forsothe that ilke Joon hadde cloth of the heeris of cameylis and a girdil of skyn about his leendis; sothely his mete weren locustis and hony of the wode. Thanne Jerusalem wente out to hym, and al Jude, and al the cuntre aboute Jordan, and thei weren crystened of hym in Jordan, knowlechynge there synnes.**

It is somewhere recorded that at a meeting in Yorkshire recently a long passage of Wycliffe's Bible was read, which was quite intelligible throughout to those who heard it.

It will be seen that this specimen is not divided into verses. Verse division belongs to a much later period,[1] and though convenient for reference, it sometimes spoils the sense a good deal. The division into chapters appears in Wycliffe's as in our own Bibles. This chapter division had shortly before been made by a Cardinal Hugo,[2] for the purpose of a Latin Concordance, and its convenience brought it quickly into use. But, like the verse division, it is often very badly done, the object aimed at seeming to be uniformity of length rather than any natural division of the subject.[3] Sometimes a chapter breaks off in the middle of a narrative or an argument, and, especially in St. Paul's epistles, the incorrect division often becomes misleading. The removal as far as possible of these divisions is one of the advantages of the Revised Version as will be noticed later on.

[1] It first appears in the Geneva Bible, 1560. See p. 122. We owe it to Robert Stephen, the celebrated editor of the Greek Testament, who hurriedly arranged it on a journey from Paris to Lyons. "I think," a commentator quaintly remarks, "it had been better done on his knees in the closet."

[2] The writer remembers the question at a Divinity examination, "Who divided the Bible into chapters?" to which a fellow student promptly replied, "Victor Hugo, sir!" "Quite right," said the examiner, whose hearing was defective.

[3] Compare, for example, the beginnings of Matt. x., xx.; Mark iii., ix.; Luke xxi.; Acts viii.; 1 Cor. xi.; 2 Cor. v., vii., &c., &c. An awkward division for a clergyman reading the lessons is at end of Acts xxi., where, however he may manage his voice, it is difficult to avoid reading, "Paul spake in the Hebrew tongue, saying, Here endeth the second lesson."

VIII.

The book had a very wide circulation. While the Anglo-Saxon versions were confined for the most part to the few religious houses where they were written, Wycliffe's Bible, in spite of its disadvantage of being only in manuscript, was circulated largely through the kingdom; and though the cost restricted its possession to the wealthier classes,[1] those who could not hope to possess it gained access to it too, as well through their own efforts as through the ministrations of Wycliffe's " pore priestes." A considerable sum was paid for even a few sheets of the manuscript, a load of hay was given for permission to read it for a certain period one hour a day,[2] and those who could not

[1] Even now, after 500 years, one hundred and seventy of these copies remain, some of them of great interest from the inscriptions on their title-pages. One bears the name of Henry VI., another of Richard, the crookbacked Duke of Gloucester, others belonging to Henry VII. and Edward VI., and one has an inscription telling that it was presented to Queen Elizabeth as a birthday gift by one of her chaplains.

[2] The readers, as might be expected, often surreptitiously copying portions of special interest. One is reminded of the story in ancient Irish history of a curious decision arising out of an incident of this kind nearly a thousand years before, which seems to have influenced the history of Christianity in Britain. St. Columb, on a visit to the aged St. Finian in Ulster, had permission to read in the Psalter belonging to his host. But every night while the good old saint was sleeping, the young one was busy in the chapel writing by a miraculous light till he had completed a copy of the whole Psalter. The owner of the Psalter discovering this, demanded that it should be given up, as it had been copied unlawfully from his book; while the copyist insisted that, the materials and labor being his, he was

6

afford even such expense adopted what means they could. It is touching to read such incidents as that of one Alice Collins, sent for to the little gatherings " to recite the ten commandments and parts of the Epistles of SS. Paul and Peter, which she knew by heart." " Certes," says old John Foxe in his " Book of Martyrs," " the zeal of those Christian days seems much superior to this of our day, and to see the travail of them may well shame our careless times."

But such study was carried on at considerable risk. The appearance of Wycliffe's Bible aroused at once fierce opposition. A bill was brought into Parliament to forbid the circulation of the Scriptures in English; but the sturdy John of Gaunt vigorously asserted the right of the people to have the Word of God in their own tongue; " for why," said he, " are we to be the dross of the nations?" However, the rulers of the Church were determined to prevent the circulation of the book. Archbishop Arundel, a zealous but not very learned prelate, complained to the Pope of " that pestilent wretch, John Wycliffe, the son of the old Serpent, the forerunnner of Antichrist, who had

entitled to what he had written. The dispute was referred to Diarmad the king at Tara, and his decision (genuinely Irish) was given in St. Finian's favor. "To every book," said he, "belongs its son-book (copy), *as to every cow belongs her calf.*" Columb complained of the decision as unjust, and the dispute is said to have been one of the causes of his leaving Ireland for Iona (see note, p. 43).

FROM A COPY OF WYCLIFFE'S BIBLE, SUPPOSED TO HAVE BELONGED TO JOHN OF GAUNT.
THE ROYAL ARMS ARE INSCRIBED ON ITS FIRST LEAF.

completed his iniquity by inventing a new translation of the Scriptures;" and shortly after, the
Convocation of Canterbury forbade such translations, under penalty of the major excommuni-
cation.

"God grant us," runs the prayer in the old
Wycliffe Bible preface, "to ken and to kepe well
Holie Writ, and to suffer joiefulli some paine for
it at the laste." What a meaning that prayer
must have gained when the readers of the book
were burned with the copies round their necks,
when husbands were made to witness against their
wives, and children forced to light the death-fires
of their parents, and possessors of the banned
Wycliffe Bible were hunted down as if they were
wild beasts.

It is difficult to estimate the silent influence of
the Wycliffe Bible during the following century
on the Church and nation of England, or how
much it counts as a remote cause of the great
movement of the Reformation. Though banned
and proscribed it must have largely leavened
the spirit of the people. There is a marvellous quickening power in the inspired Word
of God secretly working in the springs of
national life, and up to this time England
had it only in very fragmentary form. An
open Bible spreads a wholesome light in which
errors and corruptions have to flee away. It is,

to use a simile of a graceful modern writer,[1] as when you raise with your staff an old flat stone, with the grass forming a little hedge, as it were, around it as it lies. "Beneath it, what a revelation! Blades of grass flattened down, colorless, matted together, as if they had been bleached and ironed; hideous crawling things; black crickets with their long filaments sticking out on all sides; motionless, slug-like creatures; young larvæ, perhaps more horrible in their pulpy stillness than in the infernal wriggle of maturity. But no sooner is the stone turned and the wholesome light of day let in on this compressed and blinded community of creeping things than all of them that have legs rush blindly about, butting against each other and everything else in their way, and end in a general stampede to underground retreats from the region poisoned by sunshine. Next year you will find the grass growing fresh and green where the stone lay—the ground bird builds her nest where the beetle had his hole, the dandelion and the butter-cup are growing there, and the broad fans of insect-angels open and shut over their golden discs as the rhythmic waves of blissful consciousness pulsate through their glorified being.

"The stone is ancient error, the grass is human nature borne down and bleached of all its color by

[1] Oliver Wendell Holmes, in the "Autocrat of the Breakfast-table."

it. He who turns the stone is whosoever puts the
staff of truth to the old lying incubus, whether he
do it with a serious face or a laughing one. The
next year stands for the coming time.   Then
shall the nature which had lain blanched and
broken rise in its full stature and native lines
in the sunshine. Then shall God's minstrels build
their nests in the hearts of a newborn humanity.
Then shall beauty—divinity taking outline and
color—light upon the souls of men as the butter-
fly, image of the beatified spirit rising from the
dust, soars from the shell that held a poor grub,
which would never have found wings unless that
stone had been lifted."

CHAPTER VI.

TYNDALE'S VERSION.

AFTER Wycliffe there is an interval of a hundred years before we come to the next great version of the Bible, but in that interval occurred what, more than any other event that ever happened, has affected the history of the English Bible, and indeed the history of the English nation altogether. Up to this time in wild Iona, in the monasteries of ancient Britain, in the great homes of learning through the continent of Europe, men and women sat in the silence of their cells slowly copying out letter by letter the pages of the Scripture manuscripts, watching patiently month after month the volumes grow beneath their hands. But with Wycliffe's days this toilsome manuscript period closes forever.

About twenty years after the death of Wycliffe there was living in the old German town of Mentz a boy bearing the not very attractive name of Johann Gensfleisch, which means, put into plain English, John Gooseflesh. His mother was a dresser of parchments for the writing of manuscripts. One morning—so runs the story—he had been cutting the letters of his name out of the bark of a tree, and having been left alone in the house soon after, amused himself by spreading out the letters on a board so as to form again the words,

Johann Gensfleisch.

A pot of purple dye was beside the fire, and by some awkward turn one of his letters droped into it. Quickly, without stopping to think, he snatched it out of the boiling liquid, and as quickly let it drop again, this time on a white dressed skin which lay on a bench near by, the result being a beautiful purple ħ on a deep yellowish white ground. Whether the boy admired the beautiful marks on the skin or meditated ruefully of future marks on his own skin as a possible consequence history does not record, but it would seem as if somehow that image rooted itself in his mind, to bear rich fruit on a future day. For, thirty years afterward, when all Germany was ringing with the name of Johann Gutenberg, and his magical art of printing, the good people of Mentz recognized in the inventor their young townsman Gensfleisch, who had meantime taken his maternal name.[1]   Whatever truth there may be in the legend, certain it is that Gutenberg's printing press was working in Mentz about the year 1450, and the first completed book that issued from that press is said to have been the Latin Bible.[2]

This is not the place to tell what has been so often told already of the immense influence of this new invention on the progress of knowledge in the world. We have but to do with its effects as manifested in the history of the Bible, and for this it will be sufficient to remark that the Bible which took Wyckliffe's copyists ten months to prepare can now be produced by a single London firm at the rate of 120 per hour, that is, two copies every minute; while, for cost of production, we may compare the Wycliffe Bible at a price equal to £40 of our money,[3] with a New Testament complete

---

[1] He was the son of Frilo Gensfleisch and Elsie Gutenberg. The German law recognized in certain cases this taking of the maternal name.

[2] It is known as the Mazarin Bible, from the fact that a copy of it was found about a century ago in Cardinal Mazarin's library at Paris.

[3] Mr. Froude ("Hist. Eng.") has some interesting pages to show the value of money in those days. A pig or a goose was bought for 4d., a chicken for 1d., a hen for 2d.; land was let at 8d. per acre; laborers were hired at 1d. per day; the stipend of a parish priest was £5, 6s. 8d. a year; and Bradford, the martyr, writes of his fellowship at Oxford, "It is worth £7 a year to me, so you see what a good lord God is to me."

in paper covers that has lately been published for one penny!

II.

Now mark the coincidence. At the very same time, almost in the very same year, occurred another event which in God's providence largely influenced the history of Bible translation.

In November, 1454, came the invention of movable type in printing. In May, 1454, came the fall of Constantinople, and crowds of Greek scholars were driven for refuge to Western Europe, teaching the language of the rediscovered classics, and more important for this story, the language in which the New Testament was written. The great movement of " The Renaissance " had come, the revival of learning in Europe freeing men's minds from ignorance and men's spirits from blind obedience to despotism, and one of its most important factors was this revival of Greek learning.

The reader will remember that up to this time our pile of ancient " MANUSCRIPTS," *i. e.,* Scriptures in their original language, remains untouched, the earlier English Scriptures being translated, not from the original Hebrew and Greek, but from Latin versions which themselves were only translations. For many centuries Greek had been practically unknown in Western Europe but now, as has been finely said, " Greece rose from the grave with the New Testament in her hand " and before the close of the century had become an important part of University education in Europe.

And with it came the revival of the study of Hebrew. The first Greek grammar was published in 1476 and the first Hebrew grammar in 1503. Then came Erasmus, a great Greek scholar, a friend of Sir Thomas More, and set himself to the study of the best old manuscripts he could find and so gave to the world in 1516 his famous Greek New Testament. His manuscripts were not very ancient nor critically valuable. His Greek Testament consequently was not very perfect. But it was a precious boon to the Church and the precursor of a great movement in Bible translation.

III.

First (1) the Printing Press; Next (2) the revival of Greek learning; Then (3) Erasmus' Greek Testament; and now (4) at this critical period came forth the man who was to use these new powers with such marvellous effect in the service of the English Bible. In 1483, the year after the birth of Luther, and a hundred years after the death of Wycliffe, William Tyndale was born. He grew up a thoughtful, studious youth, and at an early age won for himself in Oxford a distinguished position for scholarship. Soon afterward he moved to Cambridge where Erasmus had been professor. It was just about the time when Cambridge had received the new Greek Testament. To Tyndale, who was a good Greek scholar and conversant with the Scriptures, this book of Erasmus was an inspiration. Probably it first suggested to him his design of an English New Testament translated from the original. At any rate the design was in his mind, for shortly afterward we learn that one day, in the sudden heat of controversy, he startled the company present by his memorable declaration, whose fulfillment was afterward the object of his life. "We had better," said his opponent, "be without God's laws than the Pope's." And Tyndale rose in his indignant wrath. "I defy the Pope," he cried, "and all his laws; and if God spare me I will one day make the boy that drives the plough in England to know more of Scripture than the Pope does."[1]

He had already translated some portions from the original Greek, and now, encouraged by the

[1] An edition of Tyndale's Testament, prepared during his imprisonment, is sometimes spoken of as the literal fulfillment of this vow—a Testament for the ploughboys of his native county. It contains words seemingly of a provincial dialect—faether, maester, sloene, oones, whorsse, &c. More probably, however, these peculiarities are due to a Flemish proof-reader.

report he had heard of him as a patron of the " new learning," he applied to Cuthbert Tonstal, Bishop of London, for permission to carry on his work in the episcopal household under his lordship's patronage, and with episcopal sanction. The Bishop, he says, answered him that his house was full, he had more than he could well feed, and advised him to seek elsewhere in London. He did so and was kindly received by Humphrey Monmouth, a merchant near the Tower, and in his house for nearly a year he assiduously prosecuted his task, perhaps still hoping for bishops' sanction and publishers' favour.

But he hoped in vain. It was a troubled time in the Church of England. Serious men were looking across the sea to Germany where Luther had nailed his theses to the church door and burned the Papal bull. Many in England were in sympathy with this revolt against authority and amongst them Monmouth, the protector of Tyndale, and probably also Tyndale himself. Many more dreaded it as a beginning of anarchy and schism, especially the Bishops and chief ecclesiastics. These latter would be very unlikely at such a crisis to favour the innovation of a People's Bible, especially one translated by an unknown man, perhaps even already a suspected man, and Tyndale knew well that without the sanction of the Church no publisher would dare to print his

New Testament. "Wherefore," he sadly says, "I perceived that not only in my lord of London's palace, but in all England, there was no room for attempting a translation of the Scriptures."[1]

IV.

Tyndale, however, was not one of those who, having put their hands to the plough, look back. He had determined that England should have the Word of God spread among her people by means of this new invention of printing, and he had calmly counted the cost. If his work could be done in England, well. If not—if only a life of exile could accomplish it—then that life of exile he would cheerfully accept. So in 1524 he left his native land, never to see it again; and at Hamburg, in poverty and distress, and amid constant danger, the brave-hearted exile worked at his translation,[2] and so diligently that the following year we find him at Cologne with the sheets of his quarto New Testament already in the printer's hands.

[1] Tyndale's Preface.

[2] He seems to have had no help in the translation. For correcting proofs and such work he had one Friar Roye, whom he rather humorously describes. "As long as he had no money I could somewhat rule him, but as soon as he had gotten him money he became like himself again. So as soon as I was ended I bade him farewell for our two lives, and as men say a day longer."

But a sad disappointment was in store for him. He had kept his secret well, and he hoped that in a few months more the little book would be spreading in thousands through the length and breadth of England. But just as his hopes were highest, one day there came to him a hurried message at his lodgings, and half distracted he rushed to the printer's house, seized all the sheets he could lay hands on, and fled from the town. A priest named Cochlaeus had heard an idle boast of some printers which roused his suspicions, and by diligently plying them with wine the startling secret at length came out that an English New Testament was actually in the press, and already far on its way to completion. Quite horrified at such a conspiracy, "worse," he thought, "than that of the eunuchs against Ahasuerus," he at once gave information to the magistrates, and demanded that the sheets should be seized, while he at the same time despatched a messenger to the English bishops to warn them of this unexpected danger. Hence the consternation of Tyndale and his hurried flight from Cologne.

With his precious sheets he escaped to Worms, where the enthusiasm for Luther and the Reformation was then at its height, and there at length he accomplished his design, producing for the first time a complete printed New Testament in

English.[1] Knowing of the information that
Cochlaeus had given, and that in consequence the
books would be jealously watched, he printed also
an edition in smaller size, as more likely to escape
detection, and at once made provision for the for-
warding his dangerous merchandise to England.
In cases, in barrels, in bales of cloth, in sacks of
flour, every secret way that could be devised, the
books were sent; and in spite of the utmost vigi-
lance in watching the ports, many of them arrived
and in a few years the books were scattered far
and wide through the country.

V.

Again comes before us the obvious question,
already discussed in Wycliffe's case, How does it
happen that bishops and clergy and leading religious laymen of the high type of Sir Thomas More,
opposed so strongly the circulation of Tyndale's
Bible? Be it clearly understood that we have no

[1] We have an interesting account of Tyndale's work at
Worms, from the diary of a German scholar who was a casual
visitor there in 1526. After mentioning other subjects of conversation at the dinner-table, the writer goes on to say—" One
told us that 6,000 copies of the English New Testament had been
printed at Worms, that it was translated by an Englishman who
lived there with two of his countrymen, who was so complete a
master of seven languages—Hebrew, Greek, Latin, Italian,
Spanish, English, French—that you would fancy that whichever
he spoke in was his native tongue. He told us also that the
English, in spite of the active opposition of the King, were so
eager for the Gospel that they would buy the New Testament
even if they had to give 100,000 pieces of money for it."

desire to be apologists for More or for the
Church. We are simply trying to understand a
puzzling situation. Naturally the persecuted
party at the time assumed that it was because they
were all bigoted, arrogant tyrants opposed to the
spread of the pure Gospel of Jesus Christ. Men
of those days did not usually seek to look for the
good in their opponents. Luther's enemies used
to say that because he burned the Pope's bull he
would burn the Pope himself also if he could.
Even the kindly Tyndale was roused to say that
the bishops who could burn the Gospel of Christ
would do the same to Christ himself if they had
had Him.

But practical men looking back calmly from the
distance of centuries are suspicious of such sweeping statements. They see the great opponents,
More and Tyndale, both perhaps the noblest
Englishmen of their day, both saints of God, both
martyrs who laid down their lives for conscience
sake, and they suspect that there must be something to say on both sides. Our experience of
religious and political controversies is that when
men get to know sympathetically their opponents,
they frequently find that the best of them are as
earnest about right as themselves, only with a
different conception as to what is right. It is
always well to try to understand the other man's
point of view.

VI.

In trying to think ourselves into the position of Tyndale's opponents it is necessary first to realize that in the foreground of religious thought at the time was not " the open Bible " but " the teaching Church," which held the Bible in trust for the edifying of her people. The Church was the sacred thing, the Divine Society founded by her Lord, coming down through all the ages, one body, the centre of unity, the dispenser of the Holy Sacraments, the teacher of the people in their holy faith. She was ever to keep before them the Atonement of Christ in the great service of the Mass. She was to give the appointed Scripture portions in the Psalms and Sunday Gospels. Thus had she nourished religious life in the past ages when men never thought of an open Bible and were too ignorant to use one even if they had it. That Church with all her faults was still the central fact and any disturbing of her foundations would be fatal to religion.

Such was the attitude of English Churchmen to Church and Bible in pre-Reformation days. Now the great Reformation movement was arriving. It was the result of long growing causes and tendencies in the past in which the Wycliffe Bible and the Renaissance movement had doubtless a large share. No one man originates such movements.

They " arrive " in course of time in the Providence of God. It is foolish to speak of Luther as the author of the Reformation in Germany. It is a petty sneer of Roman Catholics that the Reformation in England was the result of the shameful amours of Henry VIII. Henry had his part in bringing about the Reformation as Pontius Pilate had in bringing about the Atonement. The great flood of new tendency was increasing its pressure all over Europe and in England Henry just loosed, as it were, the floodgates and let the flood go through. At any rate it was going through. In God's good time men were going beyond the trammels and leading strings of childhood. They were ready for a fuller Bible. They had learned to think. They could see the corruptions of the Church. And now it depended on the action of the Church whether there should come a Reformation or a Revolution.

VII.

It was a critical time. Reform was " in the air." But there were two types of the men who desired reform.   One type represented by Sir Thomas More and Erasmus and Fisher, bishop of Rochester, and Colet, the Dean of St. Paul's.   They loved and reverenced the Church and sought wise, conservative reform. They deeply dreaded what seemed to them the reckless movements into which Lutheranism was growing, which tended, as they believed, to undermining authority and alienating men, not merely from the Papacy but from the organized Church itself and its ordained ministry. They did not, in theory at least, oppose an English Bible provided it was issued under proper safeguards. Erasmus, who gave the Church his New Testament in Greek, to the deep satisfaction of the English Bishops, wished also for a Bible in the language of the people, " that the husbandman might sing it at his plough and the weaver at his shuttle.[1] Sir Thomas More, the sternest of Tyndale's opponents, professed the same sentiment, but this translation, he insists, must be made by Catholic-minded men (i. e., loyal Churchmen) and at a less disturbed time and under proper Church authority, certainly not by private, unauthorized translators. Whether we agree with them or not it is surely possible at least to appreciate their position and perhaps even to believe that such men would be the wisest type of Reformers provided they could accomplish their purpose. At the same time one cannot help feeling that in the general attitude of Churchmen in their day there might be very considerable waiting for that English Bible.

[1] Preface to his Greek Testament.

The other type of Reformers were such men as Tyndale and Frith and Barnes and their friends, who in their holy zeal felt that the Bible had been kept back too long and were indignant with the Church who had failed in her duty. They were good and earnest men seeking the truth. The Church met their efforts with haughty intolerance. Naturally they felt it. It is the sad Nemesis of an unfaithful Church that her earnest sons should attempt reform in an impatient and somewhat hostile spirit. So it was with Wycliffe. So it was with Luther. So it was now, though in lesser degree, with Tyndale and his friends. Not only did they attack the corruptions of the Church, but their zeal carried them on to the undermining of its authority. Their controversial works caused much offence. Some of their religious teaching was condemned as heretical. Churchmen also remembered bitterly that in their time of peril when King Henry was trying to bend the Church of England to his wicked will, his favorite book was Tyndale's "Obedience of a Christian Man," which proclaimed the right divine of Kings over all and asserted that the Bishops had little or no right to obedience. It is easy to understand how such things should prejudice Tyndale's new Bible, all the more so that that Bible was annotated with controversial notes which were sometimes painful reading for loyal Churchmen.

'All this must be considered by the impartial reader who desires to understand fairly the position. He must remember that it was four centuries ago. Toleration is a growth of later days. Though Tyndale and his friends were in some degree to blame the whole story is a sorrowful episode in the history of the Church of England. Here was one of her sons estranged by her faults and yet withal no self-seeking demagogue but a humble, modest man, full of zeal for God's truth, such an one surely as might have been won back to his loyalty by wise, sympathetic bishops who should share with him in his longing for the highest good of the people. He openly declared that he had no wish to form a sect, that he would withdraw his book if even a worse one were set forth by authority. But it was an unsympathetic age. It had not been softened as in our day by 400 years of an open Bible. So the opposition remained.

VIII.

The Bishops made a determined attempt to stop the circulation of Tyndale's New Testament. It was no easy task. Wycliffe's Testaments had been troublesome enough, even though it took months to finish a single copy and the cost was in a great measure prohibitive. But here were books pouring into the country capable of being produced at the rate of hundreds per day, and at a price within the reach of all. Vigorous measures indeed would be necessary now!

The warning of Cochlaeus had set them on their guard, and every port was carefully watched by officers appointed for the purpose. Thousands of copies were thus seized in their various disguises, and were burned with solemn ceremony at the old cross of St. Paul's, as " a burnt-offering most pleasing to Almighty God;" [1] and still other thousands supplied their place.[2] Tyndale was but little discouraged at their efforts, for he knew that the printing press could defy them all. " In burning the book," he says, " they did none other thing than I looked for; no more shall they do if they burn me also, if it be God's will that it should be so."

It was quite clear that they could not hinder the entrance of the book into England. And then a brilliant thought occurred to the Bishop of London. He sought out Augustine Pakington, a merchant trading to Antwerp, and asked his opinion about the buying up of all the copies across the water.

" My lord," replied Pakington. who was a

---

[1] Cardinal Campeggio's letter to Wolsey.
[2] About 15,000 of his first New Testament were issued within four years.

secret friend of Tyndale, " if it be your pleasure
I could do in this matter probably more than any
merchant in England; so if it be your lordship's
pleasure to pay for them—for I must disburse
money for them—I will insure you to have every
book that remains unsold."

" ' Gentle Master Pakington,' said the bishop,
deemyng that he hadde God by the toe, whanne
in truthe he hadde, as after he thought, the devyl
by the fiste,[1] ' do your diligence and get them
for me, and I will gladly give you whatever they
may cost, for the books are naughty, and I intend
surely to destroy them all, and to burn them at
Paul's Cross.' "

A few weeks later Pakington sought the translator, whose funds he knew were at a low ebb.

" Master Tyndale," he said, " I have found you
a good purchaser for your books."

" Who is he? " asked Tyndale.

" My lord of London."

" But if the bishop wants the books it must be
only to burn them."

" Well," was the reply, " what of that? The
bishop will burn them anyhow, and it is best that
you should have the money for the enabling you
to imprint others instead."

And so the bargain was made.   " The bishop

---

[1] " Halle's Chronicle."

had the books, Pakington had the thanks, and Tyndale had the money."

" I am the gladder," quoth Tyndale, " for these two benefits shall come thereof. I shall get money to bring myself out of debt, and the whole world will cry out against the burning of God's Word, and the overplus of the money that shall remain with me shall make me more studious to correct the said New Testament, and so newly to imprint the same once again, and I trust the second will be much better than ever was the first."

The Chronicle [1] which relates the story goes on to tell that—" After this Tyndale corrected the same Testaments again, and caused them to be newly imprinted, so that they came thick and threefold into England. The bishop sent for Pakington again, and asked how the Testaments were still so abundant. ' My lord,' replied the merchant, ' it were best for your lordship to buy up the stamps too by the which they are imprinted.' "

It is with evident enjoyment that the old chronicler presents to us another scene as a sequel to the story. A prisoner, a suspected heretic named Constantine, was being tried a few months later before Sir Thomas More. " Now Constantine," said the judge, " I would have thee to be plain with me in one thing that I shall ask, and I prom-

---

[1] " Halle's Chronicle."

ise thee I will show thee favor in all other things whereof thou art accused. There are beyond the sea Tyndale, Joye, and a great many of you; I know they cannot live without help. There must be some that help and succor them with money, and thou, being one of them, hadst thy part thereof, and therefore knowest from whence it came. I pray thee, tell me who be they that help them thus."

"My lord," quoth Constantine, "I will tell thee truly—it is the Bishop of London that hath holpen us, for he hath bestowed among us a great deal of money upon New Testaments to burn them, and that hath been our chief succor and comfort."

"Now by my troth," quoth Sir Thomas More, "I think even the same, for I told the bishop thus much before he went about it."

IX.

The opponents of the book began at last to see that a printed Testament continually being produced was quite beyond their power to destroy. Bishop Tonstal profited by his lesson, and instead of buying and burning the book any longer, he preached a famous sermon at Paul's Cross, declaring its "naughtiness," and asserting that he himself had found in it more than two thousand

errors; [1] and at the close of his sermon he hurled
the copy which he held into a great fire that blazed
before him.   Sir Thomas More, whose influence
was so deservedly great in England, followed up
the attack.   " To study to find errors in Tyndale's
book," he said, " were like studying to find water
in the sea."   It was even too bad for revising and
amending, ' for it is easier to make a web of new
cloth than it is to sew up every hole in a net." [2]
Tyndale indignantly replied to this attack; and certainly his opponent does not show to advantage in
the argument, his sweeping charge narrowing
itself down at the last to the mistranslation of
half a dozen words.

Such attacks, made from different pulpits
throughout the land, were much more effective
than the previous stupid measures adopted against
the Bible, chiefly because the people could seldom
hear the refutation.   But this was not always so.
Tyndale had many sympathizers in the Church
who wanted the open Bible in England, and they
as well as Tyndale defended the book when they
could, and generally with success.

[1] " There is not so much as one i therein," says Tyndale, " if
it lack the tittle over its head, but they have noted and number it
to the ignorant people for a heresy."

[2] More's *animus* against Tyndale is amusingly shown in his
description of the translation of Jonah—" Jonas made out by
Tyndale—a book that whoso delyte therein shall stande in peril
that Jonas was never so swallowed up by the whale as by the
delyte of that booke a mannes soul may be swallowed up by the
Devyl that he shall never have the grace to get out again."

In 1529 Latimer had preached at Cambridge his celebrated sermons " On the Card," which attracted a good deal of attention, arguing in favor of the translation and universal reading of Holy Scripture. The friars were enraged, and the more so as his reasoning was so difficult to answer. At length they selected a champion, Friar Buckingham; and certainly, if he may be taken as a type of the friars of his day, the Reformers' sneers at their ignorance were not without grounds.[1] A Sunday was fixed on which he was to demolish the arguments of Latimer, and on the appointed day the people assembled, and a sermon against Bible translation was preached which to us now must read more like jest than sober argument.

" Thus," asked the preacher with a triumphant smile, " where Scripture saith no man that layeth his hand to the plough and looketh back is fit for the kingdom of God, will not the ploughman when he readeth these words be apt forthwith to cease from his plough, and then where will be the sowing and the harvest? Likewise also whereas the baker readeth, ' A little leaven leaveneth the whole lump,' will he not be forthwith too sparing in the use of leaven, to the great injury of our

[1] " They said there was a new language discovered called Greek, of which people should beware, since it was that which produced all the heresies; that in this language was come forth the New Testament, which was full of thorns and briars; that there was another new language too, called Hebrew, and they who learned it were turned Hebrews."—*Hody, De Textibus Bibl.*

health. And so also when the simple man reads
the words, ' If thine eye offend thee pluck it out
and cast it from thee,' incontinent he will pluck
out his eyes, and so the whole realm will be full
of blind men, to the great decay of the nation and
the manifest loss of the King's grace. And thus
by reading of the Holy Scriptures will the whole
realm come into confusion."

The next Sunday St. Edward's Church was
crowded to the doors, for the report had gone
abroad that Latimer was to reply to the Grey
Friar's sermon. At the close of the prayers the
old man ascended the pulpit, and amid breathless
silence the sermon began—such a crushing, scathing rebuke as Buckingham and his party never
recovered from in Cambridge. One by one the
arguments were ridiculed as too foolish for a
really serious reply. " Only children and fools,"
he said, " fail to distinguish between the figurative
and the real meanings of language—between the
image which is used and the thing which that
image is intended to represent. For example," he
continued, with a withering glance at his opponent, who sat before the pulpit, " if we paint a fox
preaching in a friar's hood, nobody imagines that
a fox is meant, but that craft and hypocrisy are
described, which so often are found disguised in
that garb."

It was evident, too, that many of the people

sympathized with the Reformers in such contests. Day by day it became clearer now that the tide of public opinion in England was setting too strongly to be resisted in favour of a " People's Bible." In spite of all opposition the book was being everywhere talked about and read. " It passeth my power," writes Bishop Nikke, complaining to the Primate, " it passeth my power, or that of any spiritual man, to hinder it now." There was no room for questioning about it. The path of the Bible was open at last. Nor king nor bishop could stay its progress now. Over England's long night of error and superstition God had said, " Let there be light! " and there was light.

X.

But the Light-bringer himself did not see that day. For weary years he had laboured for it, a worn, poverty-stricken exile in a far away German town, and now when it came his heroic life was over—the prison and the stake had done their work. His enemies were many and powerful in England, and Vaughan, the royal envoy, had been instructed to persuade him to return. But Tyndale refused to go. " Whatever promises of safety may be made," he said, " the king would never be able to protect me from the bishops, who

believe that no faith should be kept with heretics."
It is only fair to say that there is not the slightest
evidence that the English bishops had anything
to do with Tyndale's death in Germany. The
traitor by whose means he was taken was a villain
named Phillips, a clergyman of very plausible
manners, who contrived to win the confidence of
the unsuspecting exile, " for Tyndale was simple
and inexpert in the wily subtleties of the world."
He confided in Phillips as a friend, lent him
money when he wanted it and utterly refused to
listen to his landlord's suspicions about the man.
At length, their plans being ripe, Tyndale was
enticed some distance from his house, seized by
Phillips' lurking assistants, and hurried to the dun-
geons of the Castle of Vilvorden. It is pitiful to
read of the poor prisoner there, in his cold and
misery and rags, writing to the governor to beg
" your lordship, and that by the Lord Jesus, that
if I am to remain here during the winter, you will
request the procureur to be kind enough to send
me from my goods which he has in his possession
a warmer cap, for I suffer extremely from a per-
petual catarrh, which is much increased by this
cell. A warmer coat also, for that which I have
is very thin; also a piece of cloth to patch my leg-
gings—my shirts too are worn out. . . . Also
that he would suffer me to have my Hebrew Bible
and Grammar and Dictionary."

There was no hope of escape from the first. He knew that the clerical influence in England was too strong against him to hope for any help in that quarter. Long ago he had said with foreboding, " If they burn me also, they shall do none other thing than I look for," and now his foreboding was to be realized. On Friday the 6th October, 1536, he was strangled at the stake and then burned to ashes, fervently praying with his last words, " Lord, open the King of England's eyes," a prayer which was nearer to its answer than the heroic martyr deemed.

There is no grander life in the whole annals of the Reformation than that of William Tyndale— none which comes nearer in its beautiful self-forgetfulness to His who " laid down His life for His sheep." Many a man has suffered in order that a great cause might conquer by means of himself. No such thought sullied the self-devotion of Tyndale. He issued his earlier editions of the New Testament without a name, " following the counsel of Christ which exhorteth men to do their good deeds secretly." " I assure you," said he to Vaughan, the envoy of the king, " if it would stand with the king's most gracious pleasure to grant a translation of the Scripture to be put forth among his people like as it is put forth among the subjects of the emperor here, be it the translation of whatsoever person he pleases, I shall immediately make faithful promises never to write more nor abide two days in these parts after the same, but immediately repair unto his realm, and there humbly submit myself at the feet of his royal majesty, offering my body to suffer what pain or torture, yea, what death his grace wills, so that this be obtained."

Poverty and distress and misrepresentation were his constant lot; imprisonment and death were ever staring him in the face; but " none of these things moved him, neither counted he his life dear unto him " for the accomplishment of the work which God had set him.

No higher honour could be given to any man than such a work to accomplish, and among all the heroes of the Reformation none worthier of that honour could be found than William Tyndale.

XI.

And now we have to tell of the translation itself. As we have seen already, all the earlier English versions were but translations of a translation, being derived from the Vulgate or older Latin versions. Tyndale for the first time goes back to the original Hebrew and Greek,[1] though

[1] See Diagram facing the title-page. Besides Erasmus' Greek Testament, Tyndale had also before him the Latin Vulgate and Erasmus' Latin translation of the New Testament. It is said too that he used Luther's German Bible.

the manuscripts accessible in his time were not of much authority as compared with those used by our recent revisers.

And not only did he go back to the original languages seeking for the truth, but he embodied that truth when found in so noble a translation that it has been but little improved on even to the present day. Every succeeding version is in reality little more than a revision of Tyndale's; even our present Authorized Version owes to him chiefly the ease and beauty for which it is so admired. "The peculiar genius," says Mr. Froude, "which breathes through the English Bible, the mingled tenderness and majesty, the Saxon simplicity, the grandeur, unequalled, unapproached in the attempted improvements of modern scholars—all are here, and bear the impress of the mind of one man, and that man William Tyndale."

The New Testament was the work to which he chiefly devoted himself, bringing out edition after edition as he saw anything to be improved. Of the Old Testament he translated only the Pentateuch, the Historical Books, and part of the Prophets.

The margin contains a running comment on the text, and some of the notes rather amusingly exhibit his strong anti-Papal and anti-clerical feeling. He has a grim jest in the margin of Exod.

xxxii. 35, " The Pope's bull slayeth more than Aaron's calf." On Lev. xxi. 5 he comments, " Of the heathen priests, then, our prelates took the example of their bald pates; " and where the account is given, Exod. xxxvi. 5, &c., of the forbidding the people to bring any more offerings for the building of the tabernacle, he has this note on the margin, "When will the Pope say Hoo! (hold!) and forbid an offering for the building of St. Peter's Church? And when will our spirituality say Hoo! and forbid to give them more land? Never until they have all."

Many of his quaint expressions have been altered in succeeding versions, not always, perhaps, for the better. Here are a few as specimens taken almost entirely from the New Testament:

Gen. xxxix. 2—" And the Lorde was with Ioseph, and he was a luckie felowe."

Matt. xxvi. 30—" When they had said grace."

Mark vi. 27—" He sent forthe the hangman."

Rev. i. 10—" I was in the Sprete on a Sondaye."

Matt. xxvii. 62—" The daye that foloweth Good Fridaye."

1 Cor. xvi. 8—" I will tarry at Ephesus til Witsontyde."

Acts xiii. 15—" The rulers of the synagogue sent to them after the lecture, saying, If ye have any sermon to exhort the people, say on."

The fyfth Chapter.

When he sawe the people / he

W went vp into a mountaine/and when he was sett/ hys disciples cam vnto him / and he opened his mouth/ and taught them sayinge: Blessed are the povre in sprete: for theris the kyngdom of heven. Blessed are they that mourne: for they shalbe comforted. Blessed are the meke: for they shall inheret the erthe. Blessed are they which hunger and thurst for rightewesnes: for they shalbe fylled. Blessed are the mercyfull: for they shall obteyne mercy. Blessed are the pure in herte: for they shall se god. Blessed are the mayntenyers of peace: for they shalbe called the chyldren of god. Blessed are they which suffre persecucion for rightewesnes sake: for theris is the kyngdom of heven. Blessed are ye when men shall revyle you/ and persecute you/ and shall falsly saye all manner of evle sayings agaynst you for my sake. Reioyce and be gladde/ for greate is youre rewarde in heven. For so persecuted they the prophetts which were before youre dayes.

i. vi.

All these dedes here rehearsed as to norishe peace/ to shewe mercy/ to suffre persecucio/ ke not a man hap py and blessed/ nether deserve the rewarde of hev ven: but declare and testifie that we are happy and blessed and that we shall have gre ate pmocio i hev ven. and certyfy eth vs i oure her tes that we are goddes sonnes/ & that the holy gost oft is in vs, for all good thynges are geven to vs frely of god for christes bloudes sake and his merittes

TYNDALE'S NEW TESTAMENT.

Acts xiv. 13—" Brought oxen and garlandes to the churche porche."

1 Peter v. 3—" Be not as lordes over the parrishes."

Heb. xii. 16—" Which for one breakfast sold his birthright."

Matt. iv. 24—" Holden of divers diseases and gripinges."

Matt. vi. 7—" When ye pray, bable not moche."

Matt. xv. 27—" The whelpes eat of the crommes."

Mark xii. 2—" He sent to the tenauntes a servant."

Luke xx. 9—" He lett it forthe to fermers."

The following passage from Luke ii. I have selected as a characteristic specimen of Tyndale, though perhaps not showing as well as other passages would the resemblance to our Authorized Version. Opposite is printed the corresponding portion in Wycliffe's Testament, to show the growth of the English language in the meantime:

Specimen from Wycliffe.

(LUKE ii. 1-11.)

Forsothe it was don in tho dayes, a maundement went out fro Caesar August that al the world schulde be discruyed. This first discruyinge was maad of Cyryne iustice of Cirye, and alle men wenten that thei schulde make professiounech by himself in to his cite. Sothly and Joseph stighede up fro Galilee of the cite of Nazareth in to Jude, in to a cite of Dauith that is clepid Bedleem, for that he was of tho house and meyne of Dauith, that he schulde knowleche with Mary with child spousid wyf to hym.

Sothly it was don whanne thei weren there the dayes weren fulfilled that she schulde bere child. And she childide her firste born sone and wlappide hym in clothis and putted hym in a cracche, for ther was not place to hym in the comyn stable.

Specimen from Tyndale.

(LUKE ii. 1–11.)

Bit folowed in thoose dayes that there wente oute a commaundment from Auguste the Emperour that all the woorlde shulde be valued. This tarynge was first executed when Syrenus was leftenaunt in Siria. And every man wente in to his awne shire toune there to be tared. And Joseph also ascended from Galile oute of a cite called Nazareth, unto Jewry, into a cite of David which is called Bethleem, because he was of the housse and linage of David, to be tared with Mary his wedded wyfe, which was with childe. And it fortuned while they there were her tyme was come that she shulde be delyvered. And she brought forthe her first begotten sonne and wrapped hym in swaddlynge clothes, and layed hym in a manger be cause there was no roume for them within in the hostrey.

CHAPTER VII.

THE BIBLE AFTER TYNDALE'S DAYS.

I. Three Years After.   **II.** Twenty Years After.   **III.** Fifty Years More gone by.

"LORD, open the King of England's eyes!"

Pity that William Tyndale, as he gasped forth his dying prayer, could not have lifted even a little way the veil that hid from him the future of England.

I.

THREE YEARS AFTER.

In every parish church stands an English Bible, whose frontispiece alone is sufficient to tell of the marvelous change that has taken place in the meantime.

The design is by Holbein. In the first compartment the Almighty is seen in the clouds with outstretched arms. Two scrolls proceed out of His mouth to the right and to the left. On the former is the phrase, "The word which goeth forth from me shall not return to me empty, but shall accomplish whatsoever I will have done."

The other is addressed to King Henry, who is kneeling in the distance bareheaded, with his crown lying at his feet—" I have found me a man after mine own heart, who shall fulfil all my will." Henry answers, " Thy word is a lantern unto my feet."

Immediately below is the King, seated on his throne, holding in each hand a book, on which is written " The Word of God." This he is giving to Cranmer and another bishop, who, with a group of priests, are on the right of the picture, saying, " Take this and teach; " the other, on the opposite side, he holds out to Cromwell and the lay peers, and the words are, " I make a decree that in all my kingdom men shall tremble and fear before the Living God; " while a third scroll, falling downward over his feet, speaks alike to peer and prelate—" Judge righteous judgment; turn not away your ear from the prayer of any poor man."

In the third compartment Cranmer and Cromwell are distributing the Bibles to kneeling priests and laymen, and at the bottom a preacher with a benevolent and beautiful face is addressing a crowd from a pulpit in the open air. He is apparently commencing his sermon with the words, " I exhort, therefore, that first of all supplications, prayers, thanksgivings, be made for all men, for kings "—and at the word " kings " the people are

shouting, " Vivat Rex! " children who know no
Latin lisping, " God save the King! " while at the
extreme left a prisoner at a jail window is joining
in the cry of delight as if he too were delivered
from a worse bondage.[1]

This was the so-called " GREAT BIBLE " of
1539, the first English " Authorized Version."

It was indeed a marked change that had passed
over England.   The Reformation was gaining
ground among clergy and laity, Henry had openly
broken with the Pope, and there seemed no dispo-
sition anywhere to oppose the desire for a " People's Bible."

But the opposition to William Tyndale still
remained.   His writings had already been pub-
licly condemned, and the men who had condemned
him and placed a ban upon his works were resolved that his Bible should never be the Bible of
England.

Yet this " Great Bible," the Authorized Version of the nation, was virtually Tyndale's!

This is how it came about. Already in these
three years three different versions had appeared
in England. Within a few years after the appearance of Tyndale's New Testament the Church of
England had wakened to the needs of the time
and carried in Convocation, 1534, a petition for

[1] This description is taken from Mr. Froude's History of England, where, however, the frontispiece is erroneously said to
belong to an edition of the Coverdale Bible.

an English translation of the Scriptures. We may
well believe that the influence of Tyndale's Version had a good deal to do with this improved attitude. In 1535, the very year of Tyndale's imprisonment, came the Bible [1] of Myles Coverdale,
afterwards Bishop of Exeter, the man who after
Tyndale has played the most prominent part of
any in the history of the English Bible. Coverdale was a man of very different stamp from his
great predecessor. He had neither his ability nor
strength of character, nor was he, like him, fitted
by a lifelong study for his task as a translator, and
the difference comes markedly out in the work produced by each. But it is only fair to say, too, that
he was quite conscious of his defects, that he did
the work before him to the best of his ability,
" seeking it not, neither desiring it," but feeling

---

[1] Sometimes called the "Treacle Bible," from its rendering of
Jer. viii. 22, "Is there no triacle in Gilead?" Here are
some other curious expressions:—

Gen. viii. 11—" The dove bare an olive leafe in her nebbe."

Joshua ii. 11—" Our heart had fayled us, neither is there good
  stomacke in any manne."
Judges ix. 53—" And brake his brain-panne."
Job v. 7—" It is man that is born to misery like as a byrd for
  to flee."
Acts xi. 8—" Ther widowes were not looked vpon in the daylie
  handreaching."

In original edition Queen Anne is referred to as the king's
" dearest juste wyfe and most virtuous princesse." A copy now
in the British Museum has this inscription, but " Ane " is changed
to Jane, thus JAne. The other copies have, some Ane, some
Jane, while some actually leave the space blank, as if the editor
were unable to keep pace with Henry's rapid change of wives.

that his country needed it done, and modestly regretting that no better man was there to do it.

Coverdale was a man of sympathetic nature and fine literary instinct and the attractive English of his translation has considerably influenced the language of the Authorized Version. His Bible makes no pretence to be an original translation; it is " translated out of Douche and Latin into English," with the help of " five sundry interpreters " (*i. e.,* translators), and the chief of these " interpreters " is evidently William Tyndale, whom, in the New Testament especially, he closely follows.

The following year (1537) appeared " Matthews' Bible." [1] which was really prepared by John Rogers, one of the early Reformers, afterward martyred in Queen Mary's reign. His known opinions and his connection with Tyndale accounts for the suppression of his real name as likely to injure the circulation of the book. This work was Tyndale's translation pure and simple, all but the latter half of the Old Testament (which is taken, with some alteration, from Coverdale's Bible) ; and one feels pleased for the old exile's sake, though his honor was given to others, that Archbishop Cranmer should " like it better than any translation heretofore made," he " would rather see it licensed by the king than re-

[1] In it the Song of Solomon is entitled "Solomon's Balades."

ceive £1,000," and " if they waited till the bishops should set forth a better translation they would wait," he thinks, " til the day after doomsday." [1] It is not easy to understand how it escaped detection as the work of Tyndale, especially as it contained many of those strong anti-clerical notes by which Tyndale's version gave such offence.

Shortly after appeared " Taverner's Bible," [2] which was little more than an edition of Matthews' with its more violent polemical notes toned down or omitted.

None of these versions were satisfactory. Coverdale's was but a second-hand translation, and Matthews' was only in part derived from the originals, besides which the controversial notes were against its success.

So it came to pass that the Great Bible was set on foot by the Church. Archbishop Cranmer and some of the chief advisers of the king had set their hearts on having a translation that would be really worthy of its position as a National Bible. Myles Coverdale was selected to take charge of

---

[1] " Cranmer's Remains and Letters," p. 344. Parker Society.

[2] Little is known of him. The description in Fuller's " Church History," chap. ii. p. 459, is certainly not flattering—" Surely preaching must have run very low if it be true what I read that Mr. Tavernour of Water Eaton, in Oxfordshire, gave the scholars a sermon at St. Mary's with his gold chain about his neck and his sword by his side, beginning with these words, " Arriving at Mount St. Mary's in the stony age where I now stand, I have brought you some fine biscuits baked in the oven of charity and carefully conserved for the chickens of the Church, the sparrows of the Spirit, the sweet swallows of salvation."

the work, and he proceeded to Paris with the king's printer, that the book might be brought out in the best possible style.   But the Inquisitor-General got notice of the project, and the result was a repetition of the episode of Tyndale at Cologne, only that Coverdale fared better than his great predecessor, for though his Bibles were all seized by the " Lieutenant Criminall," he carried off the printing-press, the types, and the printers themselves to complete the work in England. It was published in April, 1539, and was " authorized to be used and frequented in every church in the kingdom." [1]   The reader who wants a specimen of its style has but to turn to the Psalms in his Prayer-Book or the " Comfortable Words " in the Communion Service, which are taken unchanged from the Great Bible.   It has another point of interest in connection with the Revised Version.   It indicated some texts as doubtful by printing them in small type, and among them was the celebrated passage 1 John v. 7, 8, which the recent revisers have omitted altogether. [2]

But more important to notice is the fact that the book is really no new translation.   It may be described as a compilation from Matthews' and

[1] When Henry was asked to authorize it, "Well," said he, "but are there any heresies maintained thereby?" They answered that there were no heresies that they could find maintained in it. "Then in God's name," said the King, "let it go forth among our people."

[2] See forward page 141.

Coverdale's Bibles—or better still, perhaps, as a revision of Matthews' by Coverdale; and since, as we have seen, Matthews' was almost entirely Tyndale's version, the Great Bible was really little more than a revised edition of Tyndale!

Thus had the old martyr triumphed. These men had opposed him to the very day of his death, and now here was his Bible in their midst, though they knew it not, authorized by the king, commended by the clergy, and placed in the parish churches for the teaching of the people! And as if to mark the change with all the emphasis that was possible, an inscription on the title-page told that. "it was oversene and perused at the commandement of the King's Highness by the ryghte reverende fathers in God, Cuthbert bishop of Duresme (Durham), and Nicholas bishop of Rochester." Who, think you, reader, was Cuthbert of Duresme? None other than Cuthbert Tonstal, his untiring opponent, the bishop who had turned him discouraged from his door, who had bargained with Pakington to purchase the Bibles, who had hurled into the flames from the pulpit of Paul's Cross the translation which now went forth with his own name on its title page.

II.

Twenty Years After.

It is the day of Elizabeth's entry into London, and the streets are bright with waving banners and gay dresses of the citizens struggling to get closer to the royal procession, and shouting with joy as they behold their young queen. There is more in those shouts than the mere gaiety of a holiday crowd. It is a glad day for many in England. The dark reign of Mary is over, with its imprisonments and martyrdoms, and the men of the Reformation are looking forward hopefully to the future. There are those in that crowd who have lived for years in constant dread—there are those who have had to fly for their lives, some of them companions of the exiles at Geneva, waiting to send word to their comrades abroad how it should fare in England.

Now the shouting has ceased. There is a pause in the long line of banners and plumes and glittering steel. The procession has just arrived at " the little Conduit in Chepe," where one of those pageants, the delight of our forefathers, is prepared. An old man in emblematic dress stands forth before the queen, and it is told Her Grace that this is Time. " Time," quoth she, " and Time it was that brought me hither." Beside him stands a white-robed maiden, who is introduced as "Truth, the daughter of Time." She holds in her hand a book on which is written "*Verbum veritatis*," the Word of truth, an English Bible, which she presents to the queen. Raising it with both her hands, Elizabeth presses it to her lips, and then laying it against her heart, amid the enthusiastic shouting of the multitude, she gracefully thanks the city for so precious a gift.

It was a good omen for the future of the Bible, which had been almost a closed book in the preceding reign. And within three months it was followed by one still more significant. The Reformers who had fled to Geneva returned to their homes, bearing with them a new version of the Bible, the work of the best years of their banishment,[1] and the dedication of the book was accepted by Elizabeth.

This was the first appearance in England of the famous Geneva Bible, the "Breeches Bible," as it was afterward called, from its rendering of Genesis iii. 7, where Adam and Eve "sewed fig-tree leaves together, and made themselves breeches."[2] It was the most popular Bible that had ever appeared in England, and for sixty years it held

[1] Myles Coverdale was one of them.

[2] It was really only one edition published by Barker that contained this reading, which was also the reading of Wycliffe's Bible.

its own against all rivals, for a time contesting the ground even with our own Authorized Version.

It was both cheaper and less cumbrous than the " Great Bible " of Cranmer, as well as being a much more careful and accurate work, though, like most of its predecessors, it was more a revision than a translation, being chiefly based on Tyndale. It contained marginal notes, which were considered very helpful in dealing with obscure passages of Scripture, though, as might be expected from Geneva, they were sometimes of a strongly Calvinistic and anti-church bias.* These notes should possess a special interest for us, for, as we shall see afterward, we have partly to thank them for our Authorized Version of to-day.

Some other of its peculiarities are worth notice. It was the first Bible that laid aside the old black letter for the present Roman type. It was also the first to recognize the divisions into verses, and the first to omit the Apocrypha. It omits the name of St. Paul from the Epistle to the Hebrews, and it uses italics for all words not occurring in the original.

---

* Take for example the note on Rev. ix. 3. The " locusts that came out of the bottomless pit " are explained as meaning " false teachers, heretics, and worldly subtil prelates, with Monks, Friars, Cardinals, Patriarchs, Archbishops, Bishops, Doctors, Bachelors and Masters of Artes, which forsake Christ to maintain false doctrine."

The history of the dark troublous days of opposition to the Bible and persecution to its promoters ceases forever (let us hope) with the issue of the Geneva Bible.

III.

FIFTY YEARS MORE GONE BY.

How Tyndale's heart would have swelled at the sight! A king of England himself is directing an English Bible translation!

In January, 1604, a conference of bishops and clergy had been held in the drawing-rooms of Hampton Court Palace, under the presidency of King James himself, to consider certain alleged grievances of the Puritan party in the Church, and among other subjects of discussion was rather unexpectedly brought up that of the defectiveness of the two current translations of Scripture.

England had at that time three different versions. The Genevan was the favorite of the people in general; a rival version, called the Bishop's Bible, which had been brought out some eight years after, was supported by ecclesiastical authority; while the " Great Bible " of Henry VIII.

9

Specimens.

23D PSALM.

COVERDALE'S, 1535.

The Lorde is my shepherde I can want nothing. He fedeth me in a greene pasture and ledeth me to a fresh water. He quickeneth my soule and bringeth me forth in the waye of rightteeousnesse for his names sake. Though I shulde walke now in the valley of the shadowe of death yet I feare no euell for thou are with me, thy staffe and thy shepeboke comforte me.

Thou preparest a table before agaynst mine enemies thou anoyntest my heade with oyle and fyllest my cuppe full. Oh let thy louing=kyndnes and mercy folowe me all the dayes off my lyfe that I maye dwell in the house off the Lord for euer.

GREAT BIBLE, 1539.

The Lorde is my shepherde therefore can I lacke nothing. He shal fede me in a grene pasture and leade me forth besyde ye watirs of coforte. He shal conuert my soule and bring me forth in ye pathes of righteousnes for his names sake. Yea though I walke thorowe ye valleye of ye shadowe of death I wyl fear no euell for thou art wt me: thy rod and thy staffe comfort me.

Thou shalt prepare a table before me agaynst them that trouble me: thou has anoynted my head wt oyle and my cup shal be ful. But louing kyndnes and mercy shal folowe me all the dayes of my lyfe and I wyll dwel in ye house of ye Lorde for euer.

Specimens.

23D PSALM.

GENEVAN BIBLE, 1560.

1. The Lord is my shepheard I shall not want.

2. Hee maketh mee to rest in greene pasture *and* leadeth mee by the still waters.

3. He restoreth my soule *and* leadeth me in the paths of righteousness for His Names sake.

4. Ye though I walk through the valley of the shadowe of death I will feare no euill for thou art with me: thy rodde and thy staffe they comfort me.

5. Thou doest prepare a table before me in the sight of mine adversaries; thou dost anoynt mine head with oyle *and* my cup runneth over.

6. Doubtlesse kindnesse and mercy shall follow mee all the dayes of my life and I shal remaine a long season in the house of the Lord.

BISHOPS' BIBLE, 1568.

1. God is my shephearde therefore I can lacke nothyng: he wyll cause me to repose myselfe in pasture full of grasse and he wyll leade me vnto calme waters.

2. He will conuert my soule; he wyll bring me foorth into the pathes of righteousnesse for his names sake.

3. Yea though I walke through the valley of the shadowe of death I wyll fear no euyll; for thou art with me, thy rodde and thy staffe be the thynges that do comfort me.

4. Thou wilt prepare a table before me in the presence of myne aduersaries; thou has anoynted my head with oyle and my cup shalbe brymme ful.

5. Truly felicitie and mercy shal folowe me all the dayes of my lyfe: and I wyll dwell in the house of God for a long tyme.

might still be seen chained to a stone or wooden desk in many of the country churches. But none of these was likely to be accepted as the Bible of the English nation. The Great Bible was antiquated and cumbersome, the Genevan, though a careful translation and convenient for general use, had become, through the Puritan character of its notes, quite the Bible of a party; while the Bishops' Version, a very inferior production, neither commanded the respect of scholars nor suited the wants of the people.

There was, therefore, plainly a need for a new version, which, being accepted by all, should form a bond of union between different classes and rival religious communities. Yet when Dr. Reynolds, the leader of the Puritan party, put forward such a proposal at the Conference, it was very coldly received, Bancroft, bishop of London, seeming to express the general feeling of his party when he grumbled that " if every man had his humor about new versions, there would be no end of translating." Probably the fact of the proposal having come from the Puritans had also some effect on this conservatism of the bishops; in any case it seemed that the project must fall through for want of their support.

But if the bishops in the palace drawing-room that day thought so, they soon found that they had literally " calculated without their host." There

was one man in that assembly who looked with
special favour on the new proposal, and that man
was the royal pedant who presided. A Bible
translation made under his auspices would greatly
add to the glory of his reign, besides which, to a
man whose learning was really considerable, and
who was specially fond of displaying it in theological matters, the direction of such a work would
be very congenial. And if a further motive were
needed, it was easily found in his unconcealed dis-
like to the popular Geneva Bible. The whole
tone of its politics and theology, as exhibited in
the marginal notes, was utterly distasteful to
James, as he plainly showed soon after in his
directions to the new translators, for " marry
withal, he gave this caveat, that no notes should
be added, having found in those which were an-
nexed to the Geneva translation some notes very
partial, untrue, seditious, and savoring too much
of dangerous and traitorous conceits."

Two of these notes especially vexed him. In
2 Chron. xv. 16 it is recorded that Asa " removed
his mother from being queen, because she had
made an idol in a grove"; and the margin contains this comment, " Herein he showed that he
lacked zeal, for she ought to have died," a remark
probably often remembered by the fanatics of the
day in reference to the death of James's mother,
the Queen of Scots. There was another note which

rather amusingly clashed with the grand Stuart
theories of the divine right of kings to be above
all law and to command implicit obedience from
their subjects. In the passage in the first chapter
of Exodus describing the conduct of the Hebrew
midwives, who " did not as the king of Egypt commanded, but saved the men-children alive," the
margin declares " their disobedience to the king
was lawful, though their dissembling was evil."
" It is false," cried the indignant advocate of
kingly right; " to disobey a king is not lawful;
such traitorous conceits should not go forth among
the people."

But, however men may smile at the absurdities
of James, which in some measure led to the new
translation, there can be no question as to the wisdom shown in his arrangements for carrying out
the work. Fifty-four learned men were selected
impartially from High Churchmen and Puritans,
as well as from those who, like Saville and Boys,
represented scholarship totally unconnected with
any party. And in addition to this band of appointed revisers, the king also designed to secure
the coöperation of every Biblical scholar of note
in the kingdom. The Vice-Chancellor of Cambridge was desired to name any fit man with whom
he was acquainted, and Bishop Bancroft received
a letter from the king himself, directing him to
" move the bishops to inform themselves of all

such learned men within their several dioceses as, having especial skill in the Hebrew and Greek tongues, have taken pains in their private studies of the Scriptures for the clearing of any obscurities either in the Hebrew or the Greek, or touching any difficulties or mistakings in the former English translations, which we have now commanded to be thoroughly viewed and amended, and thereupon to earnestly charge them, signifying our pleasure therein, that they send such their observations to Mr. Lively our Hebrew reader in Cambridge, or to Dr. Harding, our Hebrew reader in Oxford, or to Dr. Andrews, Dean of Westminster, to be imparted to the rest of their several companies, that so our said intended translation may have the help and furtherance of all our principal learned men within this our kingdom."

An admirable set of rules was drawn up for the instruction of the revisers, directing amongst other things that the Bishops' Bible should be used as a basis, and departed from only when the text required it; that any competent scholars might be consulted about special difficulties; that differences of opinion should be settled at a general meeting; that divisions of chapters should be as little changed as possible, and marginal references should be given from one scripture to another; and last, but by no means least, that there should be NO MARGINAL NOTES, except for the explanation of Hebrew and Greek words. This simple rule did probably more than anything else to make our Authorized Version the Bible of all classes in England, binding us together as a Christian nation by a tie which the strife of parties and the war of politics has since been insufficient to sever. Had the opposite course been adopted, we should now have probably the Bibles of different religious bodies competing in unseemly rivalry, each reflecting the theological bias of the party from which it came.

Never before had such labour and care been expended on the English Bible. The revisers were divided into six companies, each of which took its own portion, and every aid accessible was used to make their work a thorough success. They carefully studied the Greek and Hebrew; they used the best commentaries of European scholars; the Bibles in Spanish, Italian, French, and German were examined for any help they might afford in arriving at the exact sense of each passage; and when the sense was found, no pains were spared to express it in clear, vigorous, idiomatic English. All the excellences of the previous versions were noted, for the purpose of incorporating them in the work, and even the Rhemish (Roman Catholic) translation was laid under contribution for some expressive phrases which it contained.

" Neither," says Dr. Miles Smith, in the preface, " did we disdain to revise that which we had done, and to bring back to the anvil that which we had hammered, fearing no reproach for slowness nor coveting praise for expedition; " and the result was the production of this splendid Authorized Version of which Englishmen to-day are so justly proud.

For more than two centuries English Protestant writers have spoken of it in terms of almost unanimous praise—its " grace and dignity," its " flowing words," its " masterly English style." Even a Roman Catholic divine, Dr. Geddes (1786), declares that " if accuracy and strictest attention to the letter of the text be supposed to constitute an excellent version, this is of all versions the most excellent." And an almost touching tribute is paid it by one who evidently looked back on it with yearning regret, after having exchanged its beauties for the uncouthness of the Romanist versions. " Who will say," writes Father Faber, " that the uncommon beauty and marvellous English of the Protestant Bible is not one of the great strongholds of heresy in this country? It lives on the ear like a music that can never be forgotten, like the sound of church bells, which the convert scarcely knows how he can forego. Its felicities seem often to be almost things rather than words. It is part of the national mind, and the anchor of the national seriousness. Nay, it is worshipped with a positive idolatry, in extenuation of whose fanaticism its intrinsic beauty pleads availingly with the scholar. The memory of the dead passes into it. The potent traditions of childhood are stereotyped in its verses. It is the representative of a man's best moments; all that there has been about him of soft, and gentle, and pure, and penitent, and good speaks to him forever out of his English Bible. It is his sacred thing, which doubt never dimmed and controversy never soiled; and in the length and breadth of the land there is not a Protestant with one spark of religiousness about him whose spiritual biography is not in his Saxon Bible."

CHAPTER VIII.

THE REVISED VERSION.

WHILE fully appreciating the beauty and excellence of his Authorized Version, the reader who has thus far followed this little sketch will scarcely require now to ask, Why should we have needed a new revision?

He will have seen that the whole history of the English Bible from Tyndale's days is a history of growth and improvement by means of repeated revisions. Tyndale's first New Testament (1525) was revised by himself in 1534, and again in 1535. In Matthews' Bible it appeared still more improved in 1537. The Great Bible (1539) was the result of a further revision, which was repeated again in the Genevan (1560), the Bishops' (1568), and still more thoroughly in our splendid Authorized Version (1611), which latter is itself one of the best proofs of the value of Bible revision.

He will have seen also (to recapitulate here for greater clearness)—(1.) that in the present day we have access to a treasury of ancient manuscripts, versions, and quotations such as the scholars of King James's day had never dreamed of; (2.) that the science of textual criticism, which teaches the value and the best methods of dealing with these documents, has entirely sprung up since; (3.) that our scholars are better acquainted with the Sacred Languages, and able to distinguish delicate shades of meaning which were quite lost on their predecessors; and (4.) lastly, that owing to the natural growth of the English language itself many words in the Authorized Version have become obsolete, and several have completely changed their meaning during the past 300 years.

This last is more important than people think. More than 200 words have thus quite changed their meaning, *e. g.,* carriages, comfort, common, conversation, damnation, let, malice, mortify, prevent, &c.; also phrases such as "take no thought," &c. Sometimes the change of meaning is of very serious consequence. Take, for example, the word DAMNATION which now conveys to us the idea in every case of doom to a Hell of unending torment and unending sin. The English word did not mean that some centuries ago. The original Greek word means to judge or sometimes to judge adversely, to condemn, and the old

English word " damn " meant that and no more. There is an interesting example in the Wycliffe Bible in the passage about the woman taken in adultery, St. John viii. 10. Jesus says, " Woman, hath no man damned thee? " " No man, Lord." " Neither do I damn thee." That is to say, the English word *damn* at that time only meant *condemn,* without saying to *what* one was condemned. But words are dangerous things if not carefully watched, owing to this tendency to change their meaning as a language grows. For example, " He that believeth not shall be damned " would, three or four hundred years ago, have correctly expressed the meaning of the Greek. Not so to-day. The English word " *damned* " has taken on a darker meaning. Therefore we must substitute for it the word " *condemned.*" So that on account of this change of meaning as a language grows, if for no other cause, revision at certain periods will always be needed.

For all these reasons then the duty is laid upon our Biblical scholars which Tyndale in his first preface imposed on those of his own day, " that if they perceive in any place that the version has not attained unto the very sense of the tongue or the very meaning of Scripture, or have not given the right English word, that they should put to their hands and amend it, *remembering that so is their duty to do.*"

About the beginning of the last century the appearance of several partial revisions by private individuals indicated the feeling in the minds of scholars that the time for a new Bible Revision was at hand. As years went on the feeling grew stronger, and leading men in the Church were pleading that the work should not be long delayed. During the past 250 years, they urged, great stores of Biblical information have been accumulating; [1] our ability to use such information has been greatly increased; and it is of importance to the interests of religion that that information should be fully disseminated by a careful correction of our received Scriptures. Dr. Tischendorf's discovery at Mount Sinai still further intensified this feeling; and so it created little surprise when, on the 10th February, 1870, Bishop Wilberforce

[1] Fully 200 years ago the way began to be prepared for our present revision by several criticisms and attempts at correction of the Authorized Version. It soon became clear, however, that such attempts were premature in the then state of information as to the Original Scriptures, and scholars began to direct their attention rather to the laying of the foundation for a revision in the future by collecting and examining Greek and Hebrew manuscripts, together with the various early versions and quotations from the Fathers. Toward the close of the eighteenth century Kennicott and De Rossi had published the results of their examination of several hundred Hebrew manuscripts; and in more recent times the same service was rendered to the Greek by Drs. Tischendorf, Tregelles, Scrivener, and others, whose way had been prepared by many distinguished predecessors. Besides, there was the work of a long series of commentators in investigating the meaning of the Sacred Writers, so that, on the whole, a very valuable foundation for revision existed by the middle of the present century.

rose in the Upper House of the Southern Convocation to propose, " That a committee of both Houses be appointed, with power to confer with any committee that may be appointed by the Convocation of the Northern Province, to report on the desirableness of a revision of the Authorized Version of the New Testament, whether by marginal notes or otherwise, in all those passages where plain and clear errors, whether in the Greek text adopted by the translators, or in the translation made from the same, shall on due investigation be found to exist." After the enlarging of this resolution so as to include the Old Testament also, it was adopted by both Houses.

II.

Four months later, on a summer day toward the close of June, 1870, a distinguished company was assembled in the Jerusalem Chamber in Westminster Abbey.

In that room in days long gone by the first of the Lancastrian kings breathed out his weary life. Beneath those windows sat the " Assembly of Divines " when the ill-fated Charles ruled in England; here the Westminster Confession was drawn up; and here too, under the auspices of William of Orange, was discussed the great

Prayer-Book Revision of 1689, intended to join together Churchmen and Dissenters.

But no memory of that ancient chamber will eclipse in the future that of the work for which these men were assembled on that summer afternoon, for the Bible Revision had at length been begun, and this was the appointed New Testament Company.

At the centre of the long table sat the chairman, Bishop Ellicott, and around him the flower of our English scholarship. There were Alford and Stanley and Lightfoot, intently studying the sheets before them on the table. Westcott was there, and Hort and Scrivener—names long famous in the history of textual criticism—Dr. Eadie of Scotland, and the Master of the Temple, and the venerable Archbishop Trench of Dublin, with many other scholars no less distinguished than they. Different religious communities were represented—different schools of thought—different opinions on matters closely connected with the work in hand. This is one of the great securities for the fairness of the New Revision. Whatever other charges may be brought against it, that of bias, even unconscious bias, toward any set of theological views is quite out of the question where Baptist and Methodist and Presbyterian and Churchman sat side by side in the selected company of Revisers. And, as if to make this assurance doubly sure, across the Atlantic a similarly constituted company was preparing to coöperate with these to criticize the work and suggest emendations, so that on the whole nearly a hundred of the ripest scholars of England and America were connected with the New Revision.

III.

And now let us watch the Revisers at their work. Before each man lies a sheet with a column of the Authorized Version printed in the middle, leaving a wide margin on either side for suggested alterations, the left hand for changes in the Greek text, and the right for those referring to the English rendering. These sheets are already covered with notes, the result of each Reviser's private study of the passage beforehand. After prayers and reading of the minutes, the chairman reads over for the company part of the passage on the printed sheet (Matt. i. 18–25), and asks for any suggested emendations.

At the first verse a member, referring to the notes on his sheet, remarks that certain old manuscripts read " the birth of the Christ " instead of " the birth of Jesus Christ." Dr. Scrivener and Dr. Hort state the evidence on the subject, and after a full discussion it is decided by the votes of the meeting that the received reading has most

10

authority in its favor; but, in order to represent
fairly the state of the case, it is allowed that the
margin should contain the words, " Some ancient
authorities read ' of the Christ.' "   Some of the
members are of opinion that the name " Holy
Ghost " in same verse would be better if modern-
ized into " Holy Spirit," but as this is a mere
question of rendering, it is laid aside until the
textual corrections have been discussed.   The next
of importance is the word " firstborn " in ver. 25,
which is omitted in many old authorities.   Again
the evidence on both sides is fully stated, and the
members present, each of whom has already pri-
vately studied it before, vote on the question, the
result being that the words " her firstborn " are
omitted.

And now, the textual question being settled, the
chairman asks for suggestions as to the rendering,
and it is proposed that in the first verse the word
" betrothed " should be substituted for " es-
poused," the latter being rather an antiquated
form.   This also is decided by vote in the affirma-
tive, and thus they proceed verse by verse till the
close of the meeting, when the whole passage, as
amended, is read over by the chairman.

Four years afterward we glance at their work
again.   They have reached now the First Epistle
General of St. John, and the sheets lying before
them contain part of the 5th chapter.   No ques-

tion of importance arises till the 7th verse is reached—

7. "For there are three that bear record [in heaven—the Father, the Word, and the Holy Ghost, and these three are one. 8. And there are three that bear witness in earth], the Spirit, and the Water, and the Blood, and these three agree in one "—

when it is proposed that that part of the passage which we have here placed in brackets be omitted as not belonging to the original text.

Time was when such a suggestion would have roused a formidable controversy;[1] but textual criticism has greatly progressed since then, and the question is not considered by the Revisers even to need discussing. The evidence is as follows:— The passage occurs in two *modern* Greek manuscripts—one of them in the library of Trinity College, Dublin—in one or two Ancient Versions of comparatively little value, and many modern copies of the Vulgate; besides which it is quoted by a few African Fathers, whose testimony, on the whole, is not of much weight in its favor.

Against this are to be set the following facts:— (1.) Not a single Greek manuscript or church lesson-book before the fifteenth century has any trace of the passage. This in itself would be sufficient evidence against it. (2.) It is omitted in almost every Ancient Version of any critical value, includ-

---

[1] Upwards of fifty books, pamphlets, &c., written on the subject are mentioned in Horne's Introduction.

ing the best copies of the Vulgate (St. Jerome's
Revised Bible) ; and (3.) no Greek Father quotes
it even in the arguments about the Trinity, where
it would have been of immense importance if it
had been in their copies.   There is other evidence
against it also; but it must be quite clear, even
from this, that the passage only lately got interpo-
lated into our Greek Testament, and never had
any right to its place in the English Bible.[1]   The
Revisers therefore omit it from the text.

But the reader must not think that this description represents the amount of care bestowed on
the work.   After this first revision had been completed, of a certain portion, it was transmitted to
America and reviewed by the American committee, and returned again to England.   Then it
underwent a second revision, taking into account
the American suggestions, and was again sent back
to America to be reviewed.   After these four
revisions it underwent a fifth in England, chiefly

[1] Erasmus (see page 83), not finding the words in any Greek
manuscript, omitted them from the first two editions of his Greek
Testament, which was chiefly the authority that our translators
used. But as they had long stood in the Latin Vulgate, an outcry
was at once raised that he was tampering with the Bible. He
insisted that no Greek manuscript contained the passage; " and,"
said he at last, when they pressed him, " if you can show me
even a single one in which they occur, I will insert them in the
future."   Unfortunately they did find one, the manuscript of
Montfort, which is now in the library of Trinity College, Dublin,
but is evidently no older than about the fifteenth century. The
words had got into it probably from some corrupt Latin manuscript; and on this slight authority Erasmus admitted them into
his text.

with a view of removing any roughness of rendering. And there was yet a sixth, and in some cases even a seventh revision, for the settling of points that we need not enter on more fully here. So that we may have every confidence that the changes made, whatever their merits, at least were made only after the most thorough consideration.

And so the work went on, month after month, and more than ten years had passed, and some of the most eminent of those who sat that summer day in the Jerusalem Chamber were numbered among the dead, when, on the evening of November 11, 1880, the New Testament Company assembled in the church of St. Martin-in-Fields for a special service of thanksgiving and prayer —" of thanksgiving for the happy completion of their labors—of prayer that all that had been wrong in their spirit or action might mercifully be forgiven, and that He whose glory they had humbly striven to promote might graciously accept this their service, and use it for the good of man and the honour of His holy Name."

Four years afterward the Old Testament Company finished their work, and on May 5th, 1885, the complete Revised Bible was in the hands of the public.

IV.

Its reception has been disappointing. The public have largely failed to appreciate its great merits and its great value. But perhaps it is too soon yet to judge. For many years after its first appearance our present Authorized Version had to encounter fierce opposition and severe criticism—Broughton, the greatest Hebrew scholar of the day, wrote to King James that he " would rather be torn asunder by wild horses than allow such a version to be imposed on the Church," [1]—and yet in the end it won its way and attained a position that no version before or since in any country has attained.

Whether the New Version will equally succeed, or whether, as is the general opinion, it will need a revision before being fully received, remains yet to be seen. But in any case it should get a fair, unprejudiced reception. Dr. Bickersteth tells of a smart young American deacon who thought to crush it on its first appearance by informing his people that " if the Authorized Version was good enough for St. Paul it was good enough for him,"

[1] In fifteen verses of Luke iii., he says, the translators have fifteen score of idle words to account for in the Day of Judgment. With Archbishop Bancroft, who took the lead in the work, he is especially indignant. He believes that by and by King James, looking down from Abraham's bosom, shall behold Bancroft in the place of torment.

and it is to be feared that with many people who are less ignorant there is sometimes a similar spirit exhibited.

Now let us remember that, whatever the merits or demerits of the book, it is at least entitled to respect as an earnest attempt to get nearer to the truth, and to present to English-speaking people the results of two centuries of study by the most eminent Biblical scholars.

And remember, too, that no previous revision has ever had such advantages as this. Not to speak of the valuable manuscripts available, " upon no previous revision have so many scholars been engaged. In no previous revision has the coöperation of those engaged on it been so equally diffused over all parts of the work. In no previous revision have those who took the lead in it shown so large a measure of Christian confidence in those who were outside their own communion. In no previous revision have such effective precautions been created by the very composition of the body of Revisers against accidental oversight or against any lurking bias that might arise from natural tendencies or ecclesiastical prepossessions. On these accounts alone, if on no other, this Revision may be fairly said to possess peculiar claims upon the confidence of all thoughtful and devout readers of the Bible."

V.

It was objected by some, when this Revision was first proposed, that it would be dangerous to unsettle men's faith by showing them that the old Bible they so reverenced contained many passages wrongly translated, and some even which had no right to a place in it at all. It is pleasant to see that we have got more common sense to-day. It would be a sad case indeed if men's faith were ta depend on their teachers keeping from them facts which they themselves have long since known—acting, to use Dean Stanley's scathing comparison, like the Greek bishops at Jerusalem, who pretend at Easter to receive the sacred fire from heaven, and though they do not profess to believe personally in the supposed miracle, yet retain the ceremonial, lest the ignorant multitudes who believe in it should have their minds disquieted.

Far better to do what has been done—fearlessly make any changes that were necessary to remove the few superficial flaws in our Bible, and try to teach men the grounds on which such changes were made. Our faith is given to the words of the inspired writers. It is no disparagement to them if we discover that fallible men in collecting and translating these words have sometimes made mistakes, and it is certainly no honour to the words which we profess to reverence if we knowingly allow these mistakes to remain uncorrected.

When King James's translation was offered there was no such fear of unsettling men's faith, for the men of that day had already four or five different Bibles competing for their favour, and so they easily distinguished between an Inspired Original and the English versions of that original, one of which might easily be better than another.

Rightly understood, this Revision should be rather a ground for increased confidence, showing us how nearly perfect we may consider our English Bible already, when we find that this thorough criticism and the investigation of material collecting for the past two hundred years has left unchanged every doctrine which we found in our Old Version, while it certainly is helping us to understand some of them more clearly than we ever did before.

VI.

A few remarks on the New Revision itself will close this chapter. The Revisers refer to their work under the heads of TEXT, TRANSLATION, LANGUAGE, and MARGINAL NOTES.

Whatever may be thought of their corrections

of the TEXT (*i. e.,* the original Hebrew and
Greek), the reader is already in a position in some
measure to judge of the sources of information
accessible to them and of their fitness to make such
corrections.

As to TRANSLATION and LANGUAGE, perhaps
there is foundation for the charge, against the
New Testament Company at least, of having dis-
regarded the first rule laid down for them by Convocation, " to introduce as few alterations as possible into the text of the Authorized Version."
But before condemning them it is only fair to read
their explanations in the Preface. It is also
charged against them that their English is not as
smooth and graceful as that of the Old Version
to which we were accustomed. That is true. But
this at least will be universally allowed, that if we
have lost in smoothness and beauty of diction, we
have greatly gained in point of accuracy. A scrupulous attention to the force of the Greek article,
the different tenses of verbs, and the delicate
shades of meaning in particles and prepositions,
will account for many of the minor changes,
which, though they may seem at first sight trifling
and unnecessary, will often be found to affect seri-
ously the meaning of a passage. The Revisers
also claim to have avoided the practice, adopted in
the Authorized Version, of translating for the
sake of euphony the same Greek word by different

English words. For example, we have comforter and advocate—eternal and everlasting—count, and impute, and reckon [1]—as respectively renderings of the same Greek word, while, on the other hand, to take only one example, the word " ordain " represents ten different words in the original Greek. The result of such a practice is, that the English reader, using a Concordance or the marginal references of his Bible to compare passages where the same word occurs, is sometimes misled and frequently loses much useful information.

In such cases the Revisers have sacrificed elegance to accuracy of translation, though, of course, that is not a sufficient plea, unless it can be shown that elegance and accuracy cannot here go together.

The MARGINAL NOTES contain much valuable information, and often throw fresh light on the translation in the text. But it is to be regretted that in a book intended for indiscriminate circulation the Revisers have used one class of these notes rather unguardedly. When such expressions are found as " Some manuscripts read the passage thus," " Some ancient authorities omit

---

[1] In Rom. iv., Authorized Version, these three verbs are used to represent one Greek verb. Let the reader turn to the Revised Version, where the word " reckon " is used throughout the chapter, and he will see how much St. Paul's argument has gained in clearness though perhaps the passage in reading does not sound quite as well as before.

these words," &c., the reader who understands the state of the case sees nothing disturbing in the fact that out of a large number of authorities examined some few should vary from the reading found in all the others. Such readers the Revisers seem to have had in view. They did not enough think themselves into the position of the plain simple men and women who have never heard of such matters, and on whom one cannot help fearing, from the frequent repetition of such notes, they are likely to have a disturbing effect which is in reality quite unwarranted.

A very valuable improvement is the arrangement of the text into paragraphs adapted to the subject. The continuity of thought is not, as in our Authorized Version, interrupted by frequent and often very injudicious breaks into verses, while yet the facilities for reference are retained by the numbering of the old division in the margin. The printing of the Poetical Books in proper metrical form may be considered, too, a decided advantage. They were directed also to revise the headings of chapters, and it would certainly be an advantage if this were well done, adapting it to the paragraph system. But there is much force in their reason for leaving it undone. It involved in many cases expressions of theological opinion which could not fairly find a place in the Bible. Indeed, Jewish readers have had to complain of the Old Testament chapter headings in the Authorized Version, that when the prophets speak of sin it is always the sin of the Jews, but when of glory and of holiness, it is the glory and holiness of the Church.

On the whole, whatever the imperfections of the Revised Bible, and whatever its fate may be in the future, we may at the very least claim a present position for it as a most valuable commentary to the readers of the Authorized Version, placing them as nearly as an English version can do on the level with the reader of the original tongues.

VII.

But this is not to be the last stage in the history of the English Bible. Through all these centuries its language has grown in beauty, in clearness, in expressiveness, with the growth of the national life and thought and religion. It is more than any other a " National Bible," growing as the nation grew.

The German Bible is the work of one man, Luther. The English Bible is the work of many generations of Englishmen. Cædmon and Alfred, Bede and Wycliffe, Tyndale and Coverdale, handed on the torch from one generation to another, and from Wycliffe's day at least handed on the words and phrases and forms of expression which have largely influenced the making of the English language. The history of the book is interwoven with the national history of freedom and independence and personal religion. Therefore it is to us of the Anglo-Saxon race not only the Word of God but also and essentially our National Book.

But we have not yet produced our best. This Revised Version of 1880 is not our last word. It ought to have been a great success. It had more in its favour than any previous version. And yet we have to say, after thirty years, that the old Authorized Version, with all its defects, is still holding the ground, going out every year in quantities a hundred times greater than those of the Revised Version.

The Old Version holds the ground not only by the familiarity of its language but by its wonderful charm. It is universally accepted as a literary masterpiece, as the noblest and most beautiful book in the world. The New Version is more accurate, more scholarly, more valuable. But it avails not. It lacks the literary charm. The verdict of the people is, " The old is better."

On the whole we may assume that far into the twentieth century the Authorized Version will still remain the popular Bible. The version that is to supersede it will come some day, but when it does it will have more than accurate scholarship. It will have in some degree at least the literary charm and beauty which for 300 years has brought the whole English world under the spell of the old Bible.

And now we have followed the story of the Bible from the old record chest of Ephesus 1800 years ago to the Revised Version which is in our hands to-day, and it is hoped that the question has been in some measure answered, How we got our Bible.

Let the story help us to value our Bible more. It is not without purpose that God has so wonderfully inspired and preserved His message; it is not without purpose that He raised up His workers to search out the precious manuscripts from the dusty libraries of convent and cathedral, to collect and compare then together with such toil and care, and then to render into clear, graceful English for us the very message which He sent to earth thousands of years since to comfort and brighten human life. "Other men indeed have laboured, and we have entered into their labours."

May it please Him who has so preserved for us His Word to grant us all "increase of grace to hear meekly that Word, and to receive it with pure affection, and to bring forth the fruits of the Spirit"!

THE END.